Personal Best

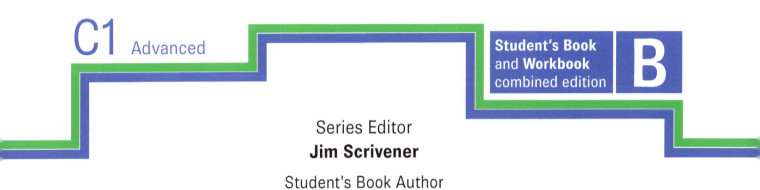

C1 Advanced

Student's Book and Workbook combined edition B

Series Editor
Jim Scrivener

Student's Book Author
Bess Bradfield

Workbook Authors
Elizabeth Walters and Kate Woodford

STUDENT'S BOOK CONTENTS

		LANGUAGE			SKILLS	
		GRAMMAR	PRONUNCIATION	VOCABULARY		
6	**A sense of community**	• the passive • using linkers	• unstressed *have* • intonation in contrast clauses	• neighbors and community • word pairs	**LISTENING** • a video about communal living • listening for agreement between speakers • sentence stress and rhythm	**WRITING** • writing a proposal • softening recommendations **PERSONAL BEST** • a proposal to improve an aspect of your neighborhood
6A	It's all in the neighborhood! p48					
6B	Co-living p50					
6C	Crowdfunding campaigns p52					
6D	Our community center p54					
5 and 6	REVIEW and PRACTICE p56					
7	**Modern life**	• verb patterns (2): reporting • future time	• consonant clusters • unstressed words in future forms	• technology • expressions with *world* and *place*	**READING** • an article about e-books and print books • understanding the writer's purpose • the pronoun *it*	**SPEAKING** • disagreeing tactfully • reaching a decision **PERSONAL BEST** • role-playing a conversation with a roommate
7A	The world is my office! p58					
7B	E-books or print books? p60					
7C	Decisions, decisions! p62					
7D	Spend or save? p64					
8	**Inspire and innovate**	• relative clauses with quantifiers and prepositions • mixed conditionals and alternatives to *if*	• sentence stress • weak forms	• science and discovery: word families • nouns from phrasal verbs	**LISTENING** • a video about concentration • identifying signposting language • changing consonant sounds	**WRITING** • opinion and discussion essays • cohesion **PERSONAL BEST** • writing an opinion or discussion essay
8A	I've found it! p66					
8B	In the zone p68					
8C	What if … ? p70					
8D	Role models p72					
7 and 8	REVIEW and PRACTICE p74					
9	**Connections**	• participle clauses • past forms for unreal situations	• intonation in participle clauses • sentence stress	• friendship and love • commonly confused words	**READING** • an article about the benefits of friendship • locating specific information • reflexive and reciprocal pronouns	**SPEAKING** • stating preferences • supporting your opinions **PERSONAL BEST** • role-playing a conversation about a dilemma
9A	Unlikely friendships p76					
9B	With a little help from my friends p78					
9C	Getting together p80					
9D	Dilemma p82					
10	**Being human**	• distancing language • adverbs and adverbial phrases	• emphasizing uncertainty • word stress	• humans and self • verbs with *re-*, *over-*, *mis-* • adverb collocations	**LISTENING** • a video looking at human achievements • understanding precise and imprecise numbers • final /t/ and /d/ sounds	**WRITING** • summarizing data • cautious language **PERSONAL BEST** • a summary of data about leisure activities
10A	Humans vs. animals p84					
10B	Breaking boundaries p86					
10C	Faith in humanity p88					
10D	A growing trend p90					
9 and 10	REVIEW and PRACTICE p92					

Grammar practice p104   Vocabulary practice p123   Communication practice p135   Phrasal verbs p150   Irregular verbs p151

Language App, unit-by-unit grammar and vocabulary games

WORKBOOK CONTENTS

		LANGUAGE		SKILLS	
	GRAMMAR	PRONUNCIATION	VOCABULARY		
6 A sense of community 6A p32 6B p33 6C p34 6D p35	• the passive • using linkers	• unstressed *have* • intonation in contrast clauses	• neighbors and community • word pairs	**LISTENING** • listening for agreement between speakers	**WRITING** • writing a proposal
6 REVIEW and PRACTICE p36					
7 Modern life 7A p38 7B p39 7C p40 7D p41	• verb patterns (2): reporting • future time	• consonant clusters • unstressed words in future forms	• technology • expressions with *world* and *place*	**READING** • understanding the writer's purpose	**SPEAKING** • disagreeing tactfully
7 REVIEW and PRACTICE p42					
8 Inspire and innovate 8A p44 8B p45 8C p46 8D p47	• relative clauses with quantifiers and prepositions • mixed conditionals and alternatives to *if*	• sentence stress • weak forms	• science and discovery: word families • nouns from phrasal verbs	**LISTENING** • identifying signposting language	**WRITING** • opinion and discussion essays
8 REVIEW and PRACTICE p48					
9 Connections 9A p50 9B p51 9C p52 9D p53	• participle clauses • past forms for unreal situations	• intonation in participle clauses • sentence stress	• friendship and love • commonly confused words	**READING** • locating specific information	**SPEAKING** • stating preferences
9 REVIEW and PRACTICE p54					
10 Being human 10A p56 10B p57 10C p58 10D p59	• distancing language • adverbs and adverbial phrases	• emphasizing uncertainty • word stress	• humans and self • verbs with *re-, over-, mis-* • adverb collocations	**LISTENING** • understanding precise and imprecise numbers	**WRITING** • summarizing data
10 REVIEW and PRACTICE p60					

Writing practice p64

UNIT 6
A sense of community

LANGUAGE   the passive ■ neighbors and community

6A It's all in the neighborhood!

1 A Complete the sentences with the phrases in the box.

on a first-name basis   come together   keep an eye on   reach out to

1 How many neighbors do you know _____ ?
2 When your neighbors are away, do you offer to _____ their house or apartment?
3 Do you _____ new neighbors and try to get to know them?
4 Have your neighbors ever _____ to improve the community in any way?

B Ask your partner the questions in exercise 1A.

Go to Vocabulary practice: neighbors and community, page 123

2 A ▶ 6.3 Listen to a podcast about neighborhoods as communities. Put the pictures in the order in which they are mentioned. Do you think the podcast gives good advice?

a

b

c

_____   _____   _____

B ▶ 6.3 Guess the missing words. Then listen again and check.

1 Most people enjoy **being called** by their _____ , and the sooner you know who's who in your neighborhood or apartment building, the better.
2 Your neighbors expect **to be treated** with consideration and _____ , and it's really the small things that make all the difference.
3 If you have a garden, keep it neat or **get** it **cared for** by a _____ .
4 As far as possible, problems should **be addressed** directly with your neighbor, rather than reported to the _____ .
5 Ask them to contact the _____ immediately if they see strangers acting suspiciously near the property. That way, your home is less likely **to be broken into**.
6 Don't forget, though, that it works both ways. If you ask your neighbors to keep an eye on your home, you **will** probably **get asked** to return the _____ .
7 Living in a close-knit community **has been** consistently **linked** to better overall health and _____ .

3 In pairs, answer the questions about the forms in **bold** in exercise 2B. Then read the Grammar box.
   1 Which sentences:
      a are passive?
      b use a form of *get*?
      c use an *-ing* form or infinitive?
   2 Which sentence means "arrange for someone to do something for you"?

48

the passive ■ neighbors and community **LANGUAGE 6A**

Grammar: the passive

get vs. be passive:
The burglar **got arrested** last night.
Parking **was prohibited** in our neighborhood recently.

get vs. have causative:
I just **got** my hair **cut**.
Could we please **have** the flowers **delivered**?

With -ing forms:
I enjoy **being asked** to help.
Being considered a good neighbor is important.
I'm afraid of **being fired**.

With infinitives:
I expect **to get evicted** soon, unfortunately.
Your house isn't likely **to be broken into**.

Look! *Get* is more informal than *be* or *have* in passive and causative structures:
Great news! I just **got offered** a job!

Go to Grammar practice: the passive, page 104

4 A ▶ 6.5 **Pronunciation:** unstressed *have* Listen to the sentences. Which forms of the verb *have* in **bold** below are stressed? Which are unstressed?

1 I **had** these pants shortened, and now they fit me really well.
2 I never fix household appliances myself. I usually **have** them fixed by someone else.
3 My neighbors **have** just **had** their house painted.
4 My brother **has** recently **had** his hair dyed. He looks so different!

B ▶ 6.5 Listen again and repeat.

5 A Complete the text with the *be* passive or *have* causative forms of the verbs in parentheses.

The first rule of dealing with neighbors

You can choose your friends, but not your family and certainly not your neighbors. Call me antisocial, but I'm OK with not knowing my neighbors on a first-name basis, and I don't mind ¹_____ (ignore) – it's better to be invisible sometimes! But I've had my share of bad neighbors. I know what it's like ²_____ (wake up) by a barking dog in the middle of the night. And I still remember all the times I ³_____ my window _____ (break) by a soccer ball. Sometimes we avoid confronting difficult neighbors because we're afraid of ⁴_____ (yell) at or ⁵_____ the door _____ (slam) in our face. But here's what I've learned about how these people should ⁶_____ (deal with): it's all about face-to-face interaction. Sometimes, a simple wave or a friendly "hello" is all that ⁷_____ (need) to break the ice. That way, when a problem arises, the fact that you've interacted before, however briefly, can make a huge difference.

B Rephrase items 1–5 in exercise 5A with *get*.

Go to Communication practice: Students A and B, page 135

6 In pairs, discuss your positive and negative experiences of neighbors. What is it about their behavior that makes them easy or difficult to get along with?

- I appreciate being …
- I don't mind being …
- I can't stand being …
- It's really annoying to be …
- It's really helpful to be …
- Having … by my neighbors is really nice.

Personal Best Write a paragraph about a good or bad experience you've had with a neighbor.

6 SKILLS LISTENING agreement between speakers ■ sentence stress and rhythm ■ word pairs

6B Co-living

1 In pairs, make a list of the main advantages and disadvantages of the following living situations:
- living on your own
- sharing a place with friends
- sharing with people you don't know
- living with your parents
- renting a place
- buying a place

2 A Complete the sentences with the phrases in the box. In which sentences do the people live with others? In which sentences do they live alone?

> bit by bit   give and take   highs and lows   time after time

1 Sometimes I wish I had somebody to talk to about the _____ of my day when I get home.
2 I've asked her _____ to do the dishes, but she never does them, and it drives me crazy!
3 When he first moved in, he was very shy and didn't say much, but _____ he became more outgoing.
4 I hardly ever got to watch my favorite shows, but there has to be some _____ – the others wanted to watch their shows, too. Now, though, I have the remote control all to myself!

Go to Vocabulary practice: word pairs, page 123

B Answer the questions in pairs.
1 What have been some of the highs and lows of your living situation?
2 Would you prefer to live alone or share, or is it not black and white for you?
3 How important is it to have an atmosphere of give and take when living with others?

3 **6.7** Watch or listen to the first part of *Talking Zone* and answer the questions.

1 What are the living situations of Sara, Tom, and Rich?
2 When Aimee explains what co-living is, which two things does she focus most on?
3 In The Village, which spaces do people share? Which are private?
4 Why does Aimee think we need co-living spaces nowadays?
5 What age group does Aimee say a lot of the residents at The Village are?

Skill   listening for agreement between speakers

Recognizing the ways speakers agree and disagree can help you understand the speakers' opinions.

- Listen for the first person's opinion, and then how the other person responds and if he/she sounds skeptical:
  I couldn't agree more!   Absolutely.   So do I.   Are you joking?   Hmm, I'm not sure about that.
- Listen to the whole response. The person may accept the other person's point, but then disagree with it. This makes the disagreement less direct and more polite:
  I see where you're coming from, but ...   That's a good point, but ...
- People often disagree by using other phrases that make the disagreement less direct:
  I'm not sure I'm completely with you on that one.
- Listen for ways people invite agreement. This signals the other person will soon respond with an opinion:
  People want to be alone sometimes, don't they?   Wouldn't you say it's true that ...?

agreement between speakers ■ sentence stress and rhythm ■ word pairs   LISTENING   SKILLS   6B

4 A ▶ 6.7   Read the Skill box. Watch or listen again. Choose the correct option to complete the sentences.
1 Tasha *enjoys sharing / likes to have her own space*.
2 Tasha thinks co-living spaces *offer / don't offer* enough privacy and tranquility.
3 Aimee thinks that *most people / only a few people* need solitude now and then.
4 Aimee thinks co-living spaces will *always / only sometimes* develop a community atmosphere.
5 Tasha thinks the sense of community is due to *the design of the space / the residents' efforts*.
6 Aimee thinks people of the *same age / different ages* should live together in co-living spaces.

B ▶ 6.7   Look at the sentences in exercise 4A. Does the other person agree or disagree with each idea? Watch or listen again and check.

5 In pairs, discuss whether you agree or disagree with Tasha and Aimee's opinions in exercise 4A.

6 ▶ 6.8   Watch or listen to the second part of the show and answer the questions.
1 How long ago does Aimee say she became a member of The Village?
2 What was her biggest problem in the houses she used to share?
3 Did Aimee like The Village the first time she visited?
4 Was The Village immediately successful?
5 By the end of the show, is Tasha interested in experiencing co-living?

7 ▶ 6.8   Watch or listen again. Are the sentences true (T) or false (F)? Correct the false sentences.
1 When Aimee first heard about The Village, she immediately wanted to move in.
2 In her previous shared housing, the buildings weren't as nice as The Village.
3 Aimee hasn't been lonely at all since moving into The Village.
4 In a recent survey, the majority of young people said they felt happy.
5 Now there are spaces belonging to The Village in Europe, too.

Listening builder sentence stress and rhythm

In English, speakers don't stress every syllable in a sentence, they stress the most important words. These tend to be "meaning" words like nouns and verbs, not "grammar" words such as prepositions and pronouns.

The more unstressed syllables there are between stressed syllables, the more quickly the unstressed ones are pronounced. This creates the stress-timed rhythm of English.
I'd like **cookies** and **cake**.   I'd like some **cookies** and some **cake**.   I'd like some **cookies**, and then some **cake**.

---

8 A Read the Listening builder. Look at the stressed words in sentences 1–5. How many unstressed words do you think there are in each blank?
1 Some _____ places _____ shared _____ great, _____ definitely highs _____ lows.
2 _____ lot _____ roommates _____ stay _____ rooms _____ play _____ phones.
3 _____ table _____ placed _____ middle _____ living room.
4 Again _____ again, people _____ told _____ difficult _____ make friends _____ big city.

B ▶ 6.9   Listen and write the unstressed words in the blanks. Then practice saying the sentences.

9 Discuss the statements below in pairs. Which do you agree or disagree with? Why?
1 Co-living sounds like the perfect solution for single people, but not for couples or families.
2 There could be a lot of problems in a co-living space.
3 Living alone makes people self-centered and inflexible.
4 It's much better to live with your family than with complete strangers.

Personal Best   Imagine you have spent a week at The Village. Write a paragraph about your experience.

6 LANGUAGE — using linkers

6C Crowdfunding campaigns

1 Imagine you have an idea for a new app, product, or service, but the initial investment is only $5,000. In pairs, list five ways that you could raise more funds for your project.

2 Read the texts below and choose the correct options to complete the sentences.

Crowdfunding involves getting *loans from banks / donations from individuals*. It can be for *business or personal projects / only personal projects*.

The Pebble smartwatch

In 2012, Pebble Technology Corporation launched one of the most successful crowdfunding campaigns of all time. They initially sought to raise $100,000 to make their first smartwatch. **However**, in a little over a month, the campaign was able to bring in an astonishing $10 million, which the company might not have been able to borrow from a bank. Therefore, Pebble became a major player in the industry and helped pave the way for Apple's smartwatches a few years later. The company was sold in 2016, though, **due to** financial problems and increased competition, ironically from the Apple smartwatch!

Joann's dream

Joann Isom, a crossing guard at the University of North Carolina, had a simple dream: visit her oldest son in the state of Arizona, all the way across the country. One day she posted her story on Facebook, and, in no time, a group of students came together and started an online campaign **so that** Joann could make her dream come true. **While** the students had set their initial goal at just $700, they went on to raise more than $7,000 on GoFundMe.com, which was probably their way of thanking Joann for all her hard work and commitment to the school.

3 Do you know any other crowdfunding success stories? Would you give money to campaigns like those in exercise 2? Why/Why not?

4 Write the linkers in **bold** in the text in exercise 2 in the correct columns of the chart below. Then read the Grammar box.

reason	purpose	contrast/comparison
because of	in order to	although
_____	_____	_____
		_____

using linkers **LANGUAGE 6C**

Grammar: using linkers

Reason:
We left *because/as/since* we were in a hurry.
The store closed *because of/due to* a lack of customers.

Result:
I had extra money, *so* I bought a new car.
The watch was beautiful. *As a result,/Consequently,/Therefore,* it sold well.
Please help me *or* I won't be able to finish.

Purpose:
They placed an ad (*in order/so as*) *to* raise funds.
I took time off *so (that)* I could take a vacation.

Contrast and comparison:
The product had positive reviews. *However/Nevertheless,* it sold poorly.
Although/Even though she stays up late, she always gets up really early.
The plan failed *despite/in spite of* my best efforts.
My sister always helps people, *whereas/while* my brother doesn't.
Unlike my parents, I never watch TV.

Go to Grammar practice: using linkers, page 105

5 A 6.11 **Pronunciation:** intonation in contrast clauses Listen to the sentences. When the contrast clause comes first, does the intonation go up (↗) or down (↘) before the comma?

1 Unlike most people I know, I hate sports.
2 Despite the weather, I enjoyed the weekend.
3 While my neighborhood isn't perfect, I like it a lot.
4 Even though I eat a lot, I don't put on weight.

B 6.11 Listen again and repeat. In pairs, make changes to the sentences in exercise 5A so that they are true for you.

6 Read the text and rewrite sentences 1–9 in *italics* using the linkers specified below the text.

Five ways to launch a successful crowdfunding campaign

¹*Crowdfunding might sound easy in theory, but it can be tricky to get right.* ²*Some campaigns may get off to a good start, but they eventually fail.* **Here are five tips:**

1 NAME YOUR PRODUCT WISELY

Your campaign should begin with a product name. ³*You may be tempted to choose a name you like, but try to pick something people will connect with.*

2 USE A SHORT DESCRIPTION

⁴*Some people have short attention spans, so they tend to skip long texts.* Your introduction should be concise. ⁵*Describe your product using two lines in a way that builds curiosity.*

3 CREATE SHORT VIDEOS WITH FURTHER DETAILS

A key feature of a successful crowdfunding page is a video that you upload. ⁶*Campaigners sometimes make it last for five minutes, but it is advisable to stick to three.* Remember: ⁷*Crowdfunding videos should end with a crowdfunding request, which ads don't need to.*

4 IF YOU HAVE TESTIMONIALS, USE THEM

⁸*Always show feedback from users on your page.* Good reviews tend to increase credibility.

5 SAY THANK YOU

Whether or not your campaign is successful, ⁹*be sure to thank your supporters.* If you don't, you might lose them.

| 1 while | 3 although | 5 so as to | 7 unlike | 9 or |
| 2 despite | 4 due to | 6 however | 8 as | |

Go to Communication practice: Student A page 136, Student B page 146

7 In pairs, create your own "Five ways to ..." guidelines. Choose one of the topics below.

Five ways to …
- be more persuasive
- save money for something special
- travel on a limited budget
- start your own business

Personal Best Choose a new topic from exercise 7 and write five ways to achieve your goal.

53

6 SKILLS WRITING writing a proposal ■ softening recommendations

6D Our community center

1 Look at the picture and read the background information. Which three activities would you be most interested in? Tell your partner and give reasons for your choices.

EAST STREET COMMUNITY CENTER is a public space where members of the community can get together for social support, public information, and many types of classes, lectures, and group activities.

Activities available include:
- after-school tutoring
- arts and crafts
- career counseling
- community picnics
- dance classes
- fitness training
- guided meditation
- table tennis

2 Read the proposal from Mark, who is on the advisory board of East Street Community Center. Choose the correct option to complete the first sentence.
  a keep our community healthy and in shape
  b increase membership
  c lower our membership fees

---

1 Introduction
The aim of this proposal is to suggest ways in which we can _____ . Our planning team is concerned about the future of our community center and wishes to consult the full advisory board in order to agree on strategies that will keep the center open.

2 Current situation
Until recently, our community center was one of the busiest in the city, largely due to its fitness room. Specifically, from 2014 to 2016, it had 504 active members, who paid $50 a month to use the facilities. However, since 2017, membership has declined by almost 40%, which has had an impact on both our image and our revenue. In order to address these issues, we e-mailed a survey to existing and former members.

3 User feedback
We received almost 200 responses. As detailed below, most users seem dissatisfied with:
- the opening hours
- the fitness equipment, namely the old treadmills and the lack of elliptical trainers
- the showers

4 Recommendations
The first [1]_____ would be to change our hours so that we're open from 6:00 a.m. to 11:00 p.m. This would be extremely beneficial to users as it would enable them to use the facilities before or after school/work, rather than only in the afternoons and on weekends. By offering more flexibility, we might be able to persuade former members to return and attract new ones of all ages.

We also [2]_____ investing in new fitness equipment, in particular, modern treadmills. Also, for us to remain competitive, it might be [3]_____ purchasing elliptical trainers, which most gyms in the neighborhood offer. It would be hard to attract new members without these machines. Please find attached price lists from three different manufacturers.

Finally, it would be [4]_____ to have all the shower heads replaced with high-pressure models, which are surprisingly affordable these days.

5 Conclusion
We are fully aware that these recommendations involve budget decisions. However, we strongly believe that these changes would improve our financial situation, as well as our appeal.

writing a proposal ■ softening recommendations **WRITING** **SKILLS** **6D**

🔧 Skill writing a proposal

A good proposal needs to be persuasive. In order to convince the reader to follow your recommendations, use these guidelines or tips.
- Begin by clearly stating your goal or purpose.
- Describe the current situation first and then make recommendations.
- Write in a more formal style. Be specific, and provide examples and details.
- Use section headings to be reader-friendly. You can use bullet points for lists.
- Include a conclusion summarizing your point of view.

3 Read the Skill box. Then read the proposal again and answer the questions in pairs.
1 Does the writer make recommendations in the first or second half of the proposal?
2 Is his style formal or informal? Specific or vague?
3 Why do you think he uses section headings?

4 Find words and phrases in the proposal that have the following functions.
1 to give more detail (section 2)   _____
2 to give more detail (section 3)   _____
3 to list specific examples (section 4)   _____
4 to list specific examples (section 4)   _____

5 Scan the proposal again and find more formal equivalents for these expressions.
1 *mostly because of* (section 2)   _____
2 *has gone down* (section 2)   _____
3 *deal with* (section 2)   _____
4 *be really helpful* (section 4)   _____
5 *know very well* (section 5)   _____

6 Fill in blanks 1–4 in the text with the words in the box below.

   advisable   recommend   suggestion   worth

🧩 Text builder softening recommendations

When writing proposals, we frequently try to soften recommendations so they are not too direct. To do this, we can use the following common expressions and verb forms.
The first suggestion would be to change our hours from 6:00 a.m. to 11:00 p.m.
*We also recommend invest**ing*** in new equipment.
*It might be worth purchas**ing*** elliptical trainers.
It would be advisable to have all the shower heads replaced.

7 Read the Text builder. Use the words in parentheses to soften these recommendations.
1 You have to offer more after-school activities. (worth)
2 Increase your social-media presence. (recommend)
3 You absolutely have to revise the budget. (advisable)
4 I'd buy new computers if I were you. (suggestion)
5 It's useless to run radio ads. (worth)

8 **A** **PREPARE** Choose a problem facing your neighborhood, such as inadequate public transportation, crime, smog, or limited shopping.

B **PRACTICE** Write a proposal from your community center to the local council. Use the Skill box to be persuasive, and expressions from the Text builder to soften your recommendations.

C **PERSONAL BEST** Exchange proposals with your partner. Are your partner's recommendations persuasive?

Personal Best Imagine you have received Mark's proposal in exercise 2. Write an e-mail to Mark with your first reaction.

5 and 6 REVIEW and PRACTICE

Grammar

1 Complete the sentences using the words in parentheses in the correct order. There is one word you don't need.

1. Rihanna's tour was (true / experience / truly / unforgettable / a).
   _____
2. Ron has (for / learning / talent / is / languages / rare / a).
   _____
3. I used to work (tall / with / man / blue / wearing / is / that / jeans).
   _____
4. My father has just baked (of / tasty / lots / cookies / to / chocolate).
   _____
5. He's the (arrested / of / shoplifting / son / woman / the / 's / for).
   _____
6. The new playroom has (small / six / tables / the / plastic / round).
   _____

2 Use the words in parentheses to complete the sentences so they mean the same as the first sentence.

1. People are treating me really badly. I'm not used to that.
   I'm not _____ so badly. (being)
2. The hairdresser has cut Paula's hair really short.
   Paula _____ really short. (had)
3. An accountant will have to check these figures for you.
   You will _____ an accountant. (get)
4. Do you ever worry that someone will break into your house?
   Do you ever worry _____ into? (having)
5. Jim was fired because he wasn't able to meet deadlines.
   Jim was fired due _____ deadlines. (inability)
6. Alana had no money, but she bought the dress anyway.
   Despite _____ the dress anyway. (fact)
7. I went to bed early so I wouldn't feel tired the next day.
   I went to bed early so _____ tired the next day. (as)
8. In spite of the rain, we went to the beach.
   Even _____ went to the beach. (was)
9. Most people I know like watching soccer on TV.
   Unlike _____ watching soccer on TV. (stand)
10. Tom is busier than ever now that he has started college.
    As a _____, Tom is busier than ever. (having)

3 Replace the words and phrases in *italics* with one word.

Before the movie
A Do you want to come over for coffee later on?
B I'd love ¹*to come over for coffee*.
A And maybe a movie afterward? How about the new ²*movie* with Emma Stone?
B I read some pretty bad reviews, but let's give it a try.

After the movie
A So, did you enjoy the movie?
B I didn't think I was going ³*to enjoy the movie*, but I ⁴*enjoyed it*.
A Me, too. You can't go wrong with Emma Stone, can you? Hey, how about some coffee now?
B Sounds great. Should we invite Mike? I really like him.
A I know you ⁵*like him*, but ...
B What?
A I think he has a girlfriend.
B Really?
A Yeah, I think ⁶*he has a girlfriend*.
B What a shame.

At the coffee shop
A I'm dying to have another piece of cake, but I don't think I ⁷*should eat more cake*.
B Oh, come on! You know you want ⁸*to eat more cake*!
A OK, then. It will help me forget about Mike.

Vocabulary

1 Which sentence has the strongest meaning, a or b?

1. a I despise her music. b I'm not a huge fan of her music.
2. a Outdoor learning appeals to kids. b Kids are wild about outdoor learning.
3. a She's a promising artist. b She's an exceptional artist.
4. a The play was tedious. b The play was appalling.
5. a I can't face seeing him. b I don't think I want to see him.
6. a I get along with my neighbors. b We're a close-knit community.

REVIEW and PRACTICE 5 and 6

2 Complete the sentences with one word. The first letters are provided for you.

1. I'm pretty obs_____ with Beyoncé's new album.
2. J.K. Rowling has always emp_____ that Harry Potter was not written specifically for children.
3. My doctor says that the media tends to exa_____ the risks of skin cancer.
4. My earliest childhood memories are usually asso_____ with food!
5. "Physical punishment can never be jus_____," experts say.
6. I'm not sure I've understood. Could you please cla_____ what you've said?

3 Complete the text with the correct verb form of the word in parentheses.

I have a great relationship with my neighbors. We know each other *on a first-name basis*, and there's a real *sense of community* on our block, with lots of *give and take*. This is especially important in this day and age, when the Internet has [1]_____ (weak) personal ties in so many ways.

I'm particularly fond of Martha, my next-door neighbor. Actually, I consider Martha one of my closest friends. She's seen me through my *highs and lows*, and time has only [2]_____ (strength) our ties. She *reaches out to* me when I have a problem, *time after time*, and that's priceless.

But we shouldn't [3]_____ (general). Not everybody is as lucky as I am. My brother's next-door neighbor plays the drums every night. To make matters worse, he's awful at it! My brother has tried speaking to him, to no avail, so lately he's been trying to figure out a way to [4]_____ (minimum) the problem, like soundproofing the house.

Personally, though, I think the other neighbors should *come together* and, *bit by bit*, try to find a more permanent solution.

4 Match the expressions in *italics* in exercise 3 with definitions a–h below.

a a shared feeling of belonging among members of a group
b gradually or a little at a time
c willing to compromise and help each other
d communicate with someone in order to help
e cooperate; work successfully with each other
f many times or repeatedly
g times that are good and times that are bad
h know people well enough to address them informally

Personal Best

Lesson 5A — Describe your favorite / least favorite artists using positive or negative verbs and adjectives.

Lesson 5A — Write two short conversations about leisure activities using ellipsis and substitution.

Lesson 5B — Find a sentence with a long subject in this book.

Lesson 5C — Name four verbs ending in -ate, -en, -ify, -ize.

Lesson 5C — Write a sentence about something unusual with information before and after the noun.

Lesson 5D — Write three sentences using expressions to speculate about the future.

Lesson 6A — Describe four characteristics of an ideal neighborhood.

Lesson 6A — Write four sentences using passives, and include a causative in two of them.

Lesson 6B — Name four word pairs and write sentences with two of them.

Lesson 6C — Name five linkers that express contrast and comparison.

Lesson 6C — Write four sentences saying why you're learning English, using linkers that express purpose.

Lesson 6D — Name two expressions you can use to soften a recommendation.

57

UNIT 7

Modern life

LANGUAGE verb patterns (2): reporting ■ technology

7A The world is my office!

1 A Read the text. What do the words in **bold** mean?

Digital **nomads**

Digital nomads are people who make a living online by working **remotely**. Instead of having a permanent home base, they move around, spending an average of 1–3 months in each different place. Usually **tech-savvy** writers, marketers, designers, or **IT professionals**, all they need is a place to stay, a device to connect to the Internet, acceptably fast **bandwidth**, and access to a reliable **wireless network**.

Go to Vocabulary practice: technology, page 124

B In pairs, discuss the advantages and disadvantages of being a digital nomad.

2 A Read the sentences about digital nomads. Guess the correct options to complete the sentences.

1 The most popular destination for digital nomads is
   a Lisbon, Portugal.
   b Chiang Mai, Thailand.
   c Medellín, Colombia.
2 Digital nomads tend to be
   a in their twenties.
   b in their thirties.
   c in their forties.
3 Generally speaking, most digital nomads
   a are self-employed.
   b have a permanent job, but work remotely.
   c own their own companies.
4 The least important requirement is
   a being computer-literate.
   b fast bandwidth.
   c a state-of-the-art computer.

B ▶ 7.4 Listen to a podcast about digital nomads and check your answers. Would you enjoy this lifestyle? Discuss in pairs.

3 A ▶ 7.5 Complete the sentences with the correct reporting verbs from the box. Listen again and check.

suggested   persuaded   asked   said

1 In the interview, I _____ Paula what it was like being a digital nomad.
2 In the end, I got the job, and they _____ I could work flexibly.
3 I was feeling pretty miserable, so my friends _____ me to spend some time abroad.
4 My sister used to live in Medellín, and she _____ I spend some time there.

B Which verbs in exercise 3A can be replaced by *encouraged* and *recommended*? Read the Grammar box.

58

verb patterns (2): reporting ■ technology   **LANGUAGE**   **7A**

 Grammar   verb patterns (2): reporting

Verb patterns:
He **said** (**that**) it **was** none of my business. (statement)
I **wondered what** she **meant**. (wh- question)
They **asked** me **if** I **would help** them. (yes/no question)
She **ordered** me **to clean** my room. (command)

The present:
She often **tells** me I**'m** unique.
My teacher **says** English **isn't** difficult.

Subjunctive uses:
I **insisted** that **he tell** the truth.
We **recommended** that **she think** about other possibilities.

Go to Grammar practice: verb patterns (2): reporting, page 106

4 A ▶ 7.7 **Pronunciation: consonant clusters** Listen to the sentences. Do you hear the sounds in **bold** in the underlined words?

1 As a kid, my parents always encourage**d** me to play sports.
2 Tom's teacher urged **h**im to do his homework more carefully.
3 I texted my boss and as**k**ed her if I could take the day off.
4 People as**k** me all the time if I can help them.

B ▶ 7.7 Listen again and repeat. Then use the underlined words to make sentences about yourself.

5 Report the conversation using only the underlined sentences.

1 Ken asked …   3 She admitted …   5 Everyone says …   7 Sue said …   9 He insisted …
2 Sue reminded …   4 Sue told …   6 Ken suggested …   8 Ken asked …   10 He urged …

1 *Ken asked Sue how things were going.*

Ken So, ¹how are things going?
Sue Just fine. ²I'm off to Lisbon tomorrow, remember?
Ken Oh, that's right. How exciting!
Sue Just between us, ³I'm having second thoughts about the whole digital nomad thing.
Ken Really? I thought you loved the freedom.
Sue Yeah, but ⁴I've been feeling a little lonely and depressed lately, and ⁵I'm such a sociable person, my friends always tell me so.
Ken Maybe you're homesick?
Sue A little, yeah. I think I miss my old, "non-nomad" lifestyle.
Ken Well, here's a suggestion: ⁶work remotely – but from home, without all the traveling.
Sue That's a possibility. But then ⁷I'll miss the excitement of life on the road.
Ken ⁸Do you think you'll ever get used to living in one place again?
Sue The thing is, I'm not sure.
Ken Well, you really have to ⁹weigh the pros and cons. Go to Lisbon, and think things over. ¹⁰Just don't rush into any decisions.
Sue I guess you're right.

Go to Communication practice: Student A page 136, Student B page 146

6 In pairs, choose one of the pairs of situations below. Discuss which option is preferable and give reasons. Then report your conversation to another group.

You can't have it both ways!

Stay close to home	OR	Become a digital nomad
Work less and make less money	OR	Work more and have a more stressful life
Eat what you like	OR	Stay in shape
Stay single	OR	Be in a relationship

Personal Best Write a paragraph about a decision you've had to make recently and the advice people gave you.

59

7 SKILLS READING understanding the writer's purpose ■ the pronoun *it*

7B E-books or print books?

1 Complete the sentences with *e-books* or *print books*. Discuss your answers in pairs.
   1 In the past two years, I've read more … than …
   2 I think … are more enjoyable to read than …
   3 I tend to focus more easily when I read …

2 Read paragraphs 1–4 of the article on page 61. Choose the correct summary below.
   a The decline of print books is inevitable.
   b Print books are neither dead nor in danger.
   c Digital reading is shrinking our brains.

Skill   understanding the writer's purpose

When reading a text, look for clues that tell you what the writer's purpose is. Texts can be written for various reasons, e.g., to inform, persuade, instruct, and/or entertain the reader.
- When a text is written to **inform** and **persuade** the reader, it often contains quotes, statistics, facts, and arguments to influence the reader's opinion.
- When it is written to **instruct** the reader, it often contains a series of steps to accomplish a specific task.
- When it is written to **entertain** the reader, it often contains a first-person perspective, engaging storytelling, and humor.

3 Read the Skill box. Then read the whole article. What is the writer's main purpose?

4 Read the article again. Are these statements true (T) or false (F)? Correct the false ones.
   1 Print books may soon be dead because bookstores like Capitol Hill Books have trouble staying in business. (Eric Weiner, the author)
   2 Holding a physical book is special because it's predictable. (Ross Destiche)
   3 The pros and cons of digital books have not been fully discussed. (David Gelernter)
   4 Most recent research suggests that people learn better when they read from screens. (Maryanne Wolf)
   5 Modern readers may have trouble focusing and concentrating, regardless of whether they read e-books or print books. (Maryanne Wolf)
   6 Readers cannot always say accurately if they learn better through digital books or print reading, so digital and print books should be integrated. (Maryanne Wolf)

Text builder   the pronoun *it*

The pronoun *it* usually refers back to a noun or idea, but sometimes *it* is grammatical and has no meaning.
Using *it* to refer back to a word or idea mentioned before:

*The book was interesting, and **it** gave me lots of ideas.* (*it* = the book)
*I read the book in an hour, and **it** was a good experience.* (*it* = the experience of reading the book)

Using grammatical *it*:
***It** is important to read the instructions carefully.*   ***It** seems unlikely that the book will ever die.*
***It** has started to rain again.*

5 Read the Text builder. Then look at the highlighted examples of *it* in the article. Which ones refer back to a word or idea? Which words or ideas do they refer to?

6 A Which examples of *it* in the sentences below refer to a noun or idea?
   1 I enjoyed / didn't enjoy the article. I thought it …
   2 When it comes to digital / print reading, I find it hard / easy to …
   3 It seems likely / unlikely that digital / print books will …
   4 It takes me … to read a whole book.

B Complete the sentences in exercise 6A so they are true for you. Discuss your ideas with a partner.

TECHNOLOGY OF BOOKS HAS CHANGED,
but bookstores are hanging in there

Eric Weiner

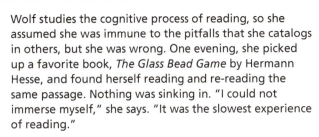

If the book is dead, nobody bothered to tell the folks at Capitol Hill Books in Washington, D.C. Books of every size, shape, and genre occupy each square inch of the converted row house — including the bathroom — all arranged in an order discernible only to the mind of Jim Toole, the store's endearingly grouchy owner.

Visitors are greeted by a makeshift sign listing words that are banned in the store, including "awesome," "perfect," and, most of all, "Amazon." The online giant has crushed many an independent bookstore — but not Toole's. "Hanging in here with my fingernails," he says with a harrumph.

Those are mighty strong fingernails, it seems. While stores like Toole's continue to struggle, independent bookstores overall are enjoying a mini-revival, with their numbers swelling 25 percent since 2009, according to the American Booksellers Association. Sales are up, too.

Remarkably, it's a revival fueled, at least in part, by digital natives like 23-year-old Ross Destiche, who's hauling an armful of books to the register. "Nothing matches the feel and the smell of a book," he says. "There's something special about holding it in your hand and knowing that that's the same story every time, and you can rely on that story to be with you."

The book also has fans from other unexpected quarters. David Gelernter, a professor of computer science at Yale, pioneered advances like "parallel computation," yet he admires the brilliant design of the codex. "It's an inspiration of the very first order. It's made to fit human hands and human eyes and human laps in the way that computers are not," he says, wondering aloud why some are in such a rush to discard a technology that has endured for centuries. "It's not as if books have lost an argument. The problem is there hasn't *been* an argument. Technology always gets a free pass. … People take it for granted that if the technology is new it must be better."

But is a digital book "better" than a printed one? The research is mixed. Some studies find we absorb less material digitally, while others find no discernible difference. One thing that *is* clear: "We are not only what we read but how we read," says Maryanne Wolf, a professor at Tufts University and author of *Proust and the Squid: The Story and Science of the Reading Brain*.

Wolf studies the cognitive process of reading, so she assumed she was immune to the pitfalls that she catalogs in others, but she was wrong. One evening, she picked up a favorite book, *The Glass Bead Game* by Hermann Hesse, and found herself reading and re-reading the same passage. Nothing was sinking in. "I could not immerse myself," she says. "It was the slowest experience of reading."

Frustrated, she thrust the book aside. It took her two full weeks to return to the sort of immersive reading she had once enjoyed. Her brain, she realized, had been altered — physically altered — by all of the scanning and flitting she had done during the day.

"For me the great lesson was that what we do at work during the day bleeds over into what we do during the night," she says. "The immersion online is always in some ways shadowed, if you will, by this constant reminder that we should be doing something else, too; that our e-mail is just a click away; that there is this almost incessant feeling of 'Well, I should go faster,' instead of 'I should immerse myself.'"

Wolf is no Luddite: she fully embraces what she calls the "bi-literate brain," one equally at home in the digital and analog worlds, but warns that e-readers can deceive us. One study found that young students, digital natives, absorbed material better on paper than on screen, even though they were convinced the opposite was true. That's why she balks at a move toward hybrid reading devices, ones that are part digital and part paper. "Better," she says, "to retain the unique advantages of both technologies."

Publishers seem to agree. They've begun to embrace the "bookiness" of their products.

"The books just look better," says paper industry analyst Thad McIlroy. He notes that publishers are paying more attention to such tactile qualities as a book's cover and the quality of paper. "Those are the kind of things that are going to keep books with us for some time to come."

codex: the earliest form of book   **Luddite:** a person opposed to technological change

Has the article influenced your opinion about paper books? Why/Why not?

7 LANGUAGE   future time ■ expressions with *world* and *place*

7C Decisions, decisions!

1 Read the two quotes below. In pairs, discuss how the two decision-making styles are different. Which style are you?

> **Leo:** It's so hard to make major decisions. I never should have thought about going abroad **in the first place**. I love living here in New York, too. I really don't know what to do.

> **Mia:** It's hard to choose a place to live these days. There are dozens of great cities, but I think I'm going to try Boston. I might regret it later, but **it's not the end of the world**.

Go to Vocabulary practice: expressions with *world* and *place*, page 125

2 Read the text below. Do you think the book was written for people like Leo or Mia?

 Read of the month:

 Brenda's blog

The Paradox of Choice, by Barry Schwartz

This might surprise you, but I'm thinking of changing jobs again. When I'm done, I'll have tried three different professions, and I'm not even 30! Yet surely having unlimited options should make my decision easier, shouldn't it?

According to Barry Schwartz, author of *The Paradox of Choice*, the answer is no. To be honest, at first, I didn't think I was going to enjoy this book, but as I read past Chapter One, and his main ideas started to fall into place, I found myself nodding in agreement all the way til the end.

The book argues that these days, we are overwhelmed by choice, from cell-phone companies to career and romance. It describes two kinds of decision-makers: "maximizers" and "satisficers," a term coined by the author. The first group looks at every possible alternative to determine the very best option, while the second goes for "good enough" and focuses on what *really* matters. Guess which group I belong to, and guess which one is happier with its choices?

The Paradox of Choice has given me more food for thought than any other book I've read this year. It reminded me that when faced with a choice, we can't always have the best of both worlds. As you may recall from last week's post, I've been considering moving abroad, but I haven't made up my mind where. So by the end of the year, I may be living in Toronto. Or Sydney. Or Johannesburg. Each city has its pros and cons, and my priorities are still all over the place, I admit. But this book has helped me realize that seeking perfection does more harm than good.

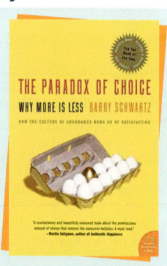

A quick thank-you note: I've just realized that next Friday, I'll have been writing this blog for five years. Time flies! Thank you so much for your continued support.

3 A Are the sentences true (T) or false (F)? Underline the parts of the text that support your answers.
1 Brenda started the book with high expectations. ____
2 She might move to Toronto this year. ____
3 When she wrote this post, she'd already had the blog for five years. ____

B Look at the parts you underlined. Which one talks about something that, in the past, Brenda thought would be true in the future? Then read the Grammar box.

future time ■ expressions with *world* and *place* | LANGUAGE | **7C**

Grammar future time

Future continuous:
We**'ll be living** in an apartment downtown.

Future perfect:
Pretty soon we **will have run out of** money.
I **will have taken** six English courses by the time I finish Personal Best.

Future perfect continuous:
By the end of May, I **will have been living** in the U.S. for a year.
She **will have been looking** for a job for six months by September.

The future in the past:
The last time I saw Tim, he **was going to** work in New York. I wonder if he's there.
Sarah **was moving** in a few weeks when I talked to her. I haven't seen her since.

Go to Grammar practice: future time, page 107

4 A ▶ 7.10 **Pronunciation:** unstressed words in future forms Listen to the sentences. Are the underlined words stressed or unstressed?

1 This time next year, I'll still be living in the same city.
2 When I go to bed tonight, I will have spent half my day online.
3 By the end of the year, I will have been studying English for four years.
4 I was going to buy a new phone, but I changed my mind.

B ▶ 7.10 Listen again and repeat. In pairs, change the sentences so they are true for you.

5 Using the verbs in parentheses, complete the sentences in Marta's journal with future forms from the Grammar box above. There may be more than one correct answer.

January 12th: I've been under a lot of stress at work lately, so last week, I asked my boss if I could take a few days off. To my surprise, she agreed! So exactly a month from today, my boyfriend and I ¹_____ (fly) to Rio. We ²_____ (stay) at his aunt's house, which means we'll be able to save on hotels and meals.

April 10th: I've been back at work for about two months now. I don't hate my job, but it's scary to think that by next month, I ³_____ (work) at the same company for ten years. I think it's time to shake things up and leave my comfort zone.

July 5th: I ⁴_____ (wait) until the end of the year to start looking for a new job, but I don't think I can take it any more. So I've been sending my résumé to lots of different companies, and hopefully I ⁵_____ (find) something by August – fingers crossed!

September 6th: Nothing yet. Next week, I ⁶_____ (look for) a new job for almost three months, which is longer than I'd expected. I ⁷_____ (quit) this week, anyway, but, on second thought, I think I should wait. I mean, what if I can't find another job?

Go to Communication practice: Students A and B, page 136

6 Tell your partner three things about yourself using the prompts below. Make <u>one</u> of the stories false. Can your partner spot the lie?

• something you're getting tired of doing because, pretty soon, you will have been doing it for too long
• something you've wanted to try for a while, and, hopefully, will have started by next month
• something you were going to do, but ended up not doing, which you've regretted
• something you were going to do, but just couldn't make a decision about

Personal Best What do you think your life will be like in 2025? Write a paragraph with three predictions.

7 SKILLS   SPEAKING   disagreeing tactfully ■ reaching a decision

7D Spend or save?

1 Which of the things below do you spend the most money on? Which would you be willing to spend less on in order to save money? Discuss your ideas in pairs.

2 ▶ 7.11 Watch or listen to the first part of *Talking Zone* and answer the questions.
1 What do Ben and Abigail disagree about?
2 What are the reasons for their opinions?

3 A Choose the correct options to complete the conversation.

Ben	We can become a TV-free household!
Abigail	I'm not so sure about ¹*this / that*.
Ben	But we hardly ever watch it!
Abigail	²*Good / Terrible* point, but I really don't think now is the best time to go TV-free.
Ben	Actually, this might be exactly the right time. They're putting our rent up again in June. Pretty soon, we'll have run out of money completely! We need to save somehow.
Abigail	Look, I totally take your ³*point / view* about saving money but … the Olympics starts in a few weeks. You know how much I love watching all the events, and I know you do, too!
Ben	Yeah, you're right. We do enjoy watching the Olympics, don't we? Mind ⁴*me / you*, we could just watch it online.

B ▶ 7.11 Watch or listen again and check your answers.

Conversation builder   disagreeing tactfully

Disagree using tentative language
I'm not so sure about that.
I'm not sure I agree …
I'm afraid I see it differently.
I'm not sure I see it the same way.

Introducing an opposite opinion
Another way of looking at it is …
Another point of view is …
On the other hand, …
Then again, …
Mind you, …

Acknowledging the opposite opinion before explaining your own
I see where you're coming from, but …
I take your point, but the way I see it, …
(That's a) valid/fair/good point, but …
Yes, but what if …

4 Take turns giving your opinions on statements 1–6. Your partner will take a different point of view, using an expression from the Conversation builder.
1 Roommates should share all bills equally.
2 People spend too much money on unimportant things.
3 Women are better than men at saving money.
4 Money can buy you happiness.
5 Money is the cause of most problems in the world.
6 The best things in life are free.

disagreeing tactfully ■ reaching a decision **SPEAKING** SKILLS **7D**

5 A ▶ 7.12 Watch or listen to the second part of the show and answer the questions.
1 Which two money-saving options do Ben and Abigail discuss?
2 What do they decide to do about the TV in the end? Why?

B ▶ 7.12 Complete the sentences. Use one word in each blank. Watch or listen again and check.

1 _____ we buy the cheapest food available, we could save over $500.
2 It's not ideal, but the _____ would be that we can then afford to replace the TV.
3 And the _____ is that we have to eat awful food all year.
4 _____ we can save money on some ingredients, without having to resort to junk food?
5 Hmm, but what _____ it's a cold winter?
6 Yeah, I can _____ the plus side.
7 That's all I have. Do you have any _____ ?
8 I like the _____ , but how much will that cost?

🔧 Skill — reaching a decision

When we need to reach a decision with another person, we can:
- suggest various options and opinions.
- invite the other person to suggest his/her ideas.
- find areas of common agreement and be open to compromise.
- discuss the pros and cons of the most attractive options and decide on the best option.

6 Look at exercise 5B again. Match sentences 1–8 to functions a–d.
a Suggesting an option   ____ ____
b Inviting others to give ideas ____ ____
c Finding areas of agreement   ____ ____
d Discussing pros and cons   ____ ____

7 Joe and Paul are planning a trip to celebrate the end of the school year. Order sentences a–i to make a conversation.

a ☐ Joe: I do, actually. Why don't we start walking to school instead of taking the bus?
b ☐ Joe: But you're already working too hard. And we have exams soon.
c ☐ Joe: That's a great idea! I've got tons of things I don't use anymore.
d [1] Joe: OK, we have three months, and we want to save $1,000 to go away. How are we going to do that?
e ☐ Paul: Well it would be good to get some exercise! But it would only save us a little bit of money.
f ☐ Paul: My boss said I could do some more shifts at the restaurant.
g ☐ Paul: We could make the rest of the money by selling things online that we don't need.
h ☐ Paul: Yeah, you're probably right. I already feel too tired to study. Do you have any ideas?
i ☐ Joe: It's a start, though, isn't it? What else could we do?

Go to Communication practice: Student A page 137, Student B page 147

8 A PREPARE In pairs, imagine you share an apartment with another person, and the rent is about to go up. Make a list of ways you could save money.

B PRACTICE Find a different partner. Decide on the best two ways to save money. When your partner suggests an option you don't like, remember to disagree tactfully.

C PERSONAL BEST Did you reach a decision and disagree tactfully on options you didn't like? Find a different partner and decide on just one way to save money.

Personal Best Write a short conversation between you and a friend deciding what to do tonight.

UNIT 8 Inspire and innovate

LANGUAGE relative clauses with quantifiers and prepositions ■ science and discovery

8A I've found it!

1 How many famous scientists do you know? What are they famous for? Discuss in pairs.

2 A Read the text below. Does the writer agree with the quotation from Edison?

EUREKA! The truth behind those moments of inspiration

History is full of stories suggesting that scientific breakthroughs happen suddenly, in a flash of inspiration. Perhaps the most famous of these concerns Isaac Newton, a physicist, who was supposedly sitting under a tree in his mother's garden when an apple fell on his head. Thanks to this, Newton came up with his theory of gravity.

Nearly two thousand years earlier, the mathematician and physicist Archimedes was struggling with a problem that nobody could find the answer to – how to accurately measure the volume of an object. When he noticed the water in his bathtub rising as he got in, the solution came to him. "Eureka!" he reportedly proclaimed, which means "I've found it" in Ancient Greek. Apparently, he was so excited by his discovery, which became very influential, that he jumped out of the bathtub and ran naked into the street to tell everyone!

These two stories, both of which involve scientists suddenly solving problems that they'd been working on, have been told for centuries. People enjoy the simplicity of them, and we like the images of an apple falling from a tree or an old man jumping out of the bathtub. Perhaps they even lead us to believe that we too can make great discoveries if we're lucky enough to have our own "Eureka moment." But, in reality, such discoveries usually follow years of hard work and serious scientific analysis, most of which isn't of interest to people in the same way as the two stories mentioned previously.

Recent studies suggest that effective problem-solving often requires two types of attention. The first stage is analytical thinking, which involves paying close attention to detail. This stage may take years or even decades. But there comes a point when we must step away from the problem and give it space and time. And it's during this less focused stage, when we're in the bathtub, or under an apple tree, that our Eureka moments are more likely to come.

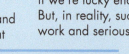

"Genius is 1% inspiration and 99% perspiration."
Thomas Edison, inventor of the light bulb

B Answer the questions in pairs.
1 Had you heard the two Eureka-moment stories in the text before? Do you think they're true?
2 Have you ever had a Eureka moment, when a solution to a problem suddenly came to you?

3 Complete the sentences from the text with the noun or adjective form of the verbs in parentheses.
1 Scientific breakthroughs happen suddenly, in a flash of _____ . (inspire)
2 Newton came up with his _____ of gravity. (theorize)
3 He was so excited by his discovery, which became very _____ . (influence)
4 The first stage is _____ thinking, which involves paying close attention to detail. (analyze)

Go to Vocabulary practice: science and discovery: word families, page 125

4 A Match the two parts of the sentence below. Then check your answers in the text.

1 History is full of stories
2 The most famous of these concerns Newton,
3 The mathematician and physicist Archimedes was struggling with a problem
4 Such discoveries usually follow years of hard work and serious scientific analysis,

a who was sitting under a tree when an apple fell on his head.
b most of which isn't of interest to people.
c suggesting that scientific breakthroughs happen suddenly.
d that nobody could find the answer to.

relative clauses with quantifiers and prepositions ■ science and discovery   **LANGUAGE**   **8A**

B Look at relative clauses a–d in exercise 4A and answer the questions below. Then read the Grammar box.
1 Which identify the subject? Which give extra information?
2 Which has a quantifier before the relative pronoun?
3 Which has a preposition at the end of the clause?

📖 **Grammar** relative clauses with quantifiers and prepositions

Non-defining relative clauses with quantifiers:
He has three jobs, **none of which** are full-time.
I have 20 classmates, **most of whom** will pass.

Relative clauses with prepositions:
He's busy with the project that he's working **on**.
She's fond of the people who she lives **with**.

Look! In formal English, the preposition comes <u>before</u> the relative pronoun.
She's fond of the people **with whom** she lives.

Go to Grammar practice: relative clauses with quantifiers and prepositions, page 108

5 ▶8.3 **Pronunciation:** sentence stress Listen to the sentences. <u>Underline</u> the stressed words in the phrases in **bold**. Then listen again and repeat.
1 I have over twenty cousins, **most of whom** live in Canada.
2 He made some good points, which were hard to **argue with**.
3 There's a lot of information here, **some of which** is not relevant.
4 She wrote me a long message that I haven't yet **replied to**.
5 They have four children, **all of whom** look like their father.
6 Graduating from college is something that I'm really **proud of**.

6 A ▶8.4 Listen to three people talking about moments of inspiration. Complete the notes with no more than three words. Which solution do you like best?

Pavel
Problem: lost his _____
Solution: _____ for money

Elena
Problem: isn't good at _____
Solution: served _____

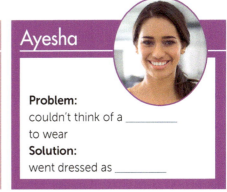

Ayesha
Problem: couldn't think of a _____ to wear
Solution: went dressed as _____

B ▶8.4 Listen again. Complete the relative clauses with a quantifier phrase that matches the information.
1 The street was full of people, _____ completely ignored Pavel.
2 His music caught the attention of some people, _____ started dancing.
3 Elena served her friends a lot of food, _____ she'd cooked herself.
4 The takeout food came in boxes, _____ she'd forgotten to throw away.
5 Ayesha wore a shirt, pants, sneakers, and a baseball cap, _____ were white.
6 Her costume confused the other guests, _____ had gone as Picasso.

Go to Communication practice: Student A page 137, Student B page 147

7 Make sentences with relative clauses using the phrases below. In pairs, discuss the sentences.
My brother is someone who I've always been able to rely on when I'm in trouble.

rely on | care about | vote for | complain about | proud of | insist on | addicted to
fed up with | focus on | disapprove of | confused about | suspicious of

Personal Best Write a paragraph about a time when you were inspired.

67

8   SKILLS   LISTENING   signposting ■ changing consonant sounds ■ nouns from phrasal verbs

8B In the zone

1 Look at the pictures. What helps you stay focused when you do these activities? What distracts you?

working to a deadline

doing a hobby / leisure activity

working out / playing sports

2 A Read two people's answers to the questions in exercise 1. Are they similar to your answers?

> I find it fairly easy to focus when I'm having a ^{1}**workout**. Thinking about my fitness goals helps me stay focused. I usually turn my phone off, as I'm easily distracted by all the alerts I get. I don't get to go to the gym often, so when it comes to staying in shape, I'm always playing ^{2}**catch-up**.

> I find it pretty hard to focus when I'm working to a deadline. Making a ^{3}**breakdown** of all the tasks I have to do helps me focus and stay on track. I get distracted by anything that's happening in my life. I was really upset about a ^{4}**breakup** last month, and I couldn't focus at all.

B Look at exercise 2A. What do the words 1–4 mean? Compare your ideas in pairs.

Go to Vocabulary practice: nouns from phrasal verbs, page 126

3 Answer the questions in pairs.
1 What kind of giveaways make it more likely for you to use or buy a product?
2 How often do you have a good workout?
3 If you could make a backup of only one file, what would it be?

4 8.6 Watch or listen to the first part of *Talking Zone*. Are the sentences true (T) or false (F)? Correct the false sentences.

1 "The zone" is an effortless period of intense concentration.
2 Duncan first noticed the zone when he saw his friend playing guitar.
3 The zone, or "flow," is a recently discovered phenomenon.
4 Duncan thinks it's easier to get into the zone nowadays as there are fewer distractions in our lives.

Skill   identifying signposting language

Recognizing signposting language helps us anticipate and follow what someone is saying. Listen for the following language:

- Phrases that introduce a point or topic, or refer back to one, e.g.,
  my point is this, incidentally, now let's consider, as I said earlier
- Phrases that show that a speaker is going to rephrase and repeat something, e.g.,
  let me put it this way, in other words, to recap
- Phrases that signpost a point in a sequence or a conclusion, e.g.,
  for starters, then you … , and then lastly, so to sum up, so it's clear from what we've said that
- Questions that introduce an explanation, e.g., *What does that mean for … ? Where does that lead us?*

signposting ■ changing consonant sounds ■ nouns from phrasal verbs   LISTENING   SKILLS   8B

5 A ▶ 8.6 Read the Skill box. Watch or listen again. Complete the extracts with the phrases in the box.

> as I've already mentioned   for starters   let me put it this way   let's turn to
> moving on to   my point is this   so, to sum up   what does this mean for us

1 Yes, exactly. Although, _____ , people call it different things.
2 _____ , it was a major part of many ancient philosophies.
3 But whatever you call it, _____ : the idea is always the same.
4 And _____ today – is the zone still important?
5 _____ – have you tried to completely focus on one thing lately?
6 But _____ ? What are we losing, if we're unable to find our flow?
7 _____ , your question is "can we still find the zone"?
8 _____ that in part two.

B Which phrases in exercise 5A introduce a point or topic? Which phrase refers to an earlier point?

6 Have you ever been in the zone? What were you doing? What was it like?

7 ▶ 8.7 Watch or listen to the second part. Complete the summary with one word in each blank.

> Duncan Jennings specializes in the study of flow, which is a state that he says everyone can experience. Psychologists have made a [1]_____ of the necessary conditions for this state to occur. First, the activity can't be too easy. It needs to [2]_____ you enough. Second, you must have the necessary [3]_____ to do the activity – education and knowledge are still vital. And third, you need to be free from [4]_____ .

8 A ▶ 8.7 Watch or listen again. Answer the questions.
1 When was the term "flow" first used?
2 With which group of professionals did psychologists first notice the state of flow?
3 What is flow unable to give you, according to Duncan?
4 What worries Duncan about the modern world?
5 Which three examples does he give of professions that require flow?

B In pairs, think of three other professions for which being in the zone is important.

Listening builder | changing consonant sounds

When a word ending in a /t/ or /d/ sound is followed by a word beginning with a /y/ sound, the /t/ or /d/ sound can change
- The /t/ sound can become a /tʃ/ sound (like the "ch" in "cheese").
  *Have you finished? No**t y**et.*
- The /d/ sound can become a /dʒ/ sound (like the "j" in "jump").
  *Woul**d y**ou like coffee?*

9 A Read the Listening builder. Then mark where the /tʃ/ and /dʒ/ sounds are in the two questions.
1 Without a doubt – I mean, aren't you?
2 Could you imagine a world where people couldn't zone in?

B ▶ 8.8 Listen and check. Then practice saying the two questions.

10 Discuss the questions in pairs.
1 Which three activities would you really love to be able to get in the zone for (even if you don't have the skills to do them yet)?
2 What would be your dream profession? Is it a profession that would really benefit from a state of flow?

Personal Best Imagine you have created a space where you can focus on something for hours. Write a paragraph about it.

8 LANGUAGE   mixed conditionals and alternatives to *if*

8C What if …?

1 What are the most useful recent inventions? In pairs, agree on the top five.

2 Read the introduction to an article about new inventions. Do you agree with the writer? Why/Why not?

What's the use?

What if the computer chip had never been invented? Nobody can argue against the importance of invention. After all, [1]if we don't innovate, we don't progress as a society. And, of course, some inventions from history have been hugely influential and useful. Some have saved countless lives. For example, [2]if the microscope hadn't been invented around 400 years ago, scientists wouldn't have been able to learn about diseases and how to treat them. But these days, are we simply inventing things for the sake of it? [3]If nobody invented a new smartphone ever again, would it make any difference to us as a society? Of course not. And yet, [4]if a new version of smartphone goes on sale tomorrow, people will line up for hours to buy it! I believe we've lost perspective, and we need to consider how much modern inventions actually benefit our lives.

3 Match sentences 1–4 from the article with the types of conditionals, a–d below.

a zero conditional   _____
b first conditional _____
c second conditional _____
d third conditional _____

4 A ▶ 8.9   Listen to three people talking about recent inventions and complete the chart.

	invention	why it's useful to the speaker
Speaker 1		
Speaker 2		
Speaker 3		

B Which inventions have made the most difference in your life? Discuss in pairs.

5 A ▶ 8.9   Listen and complete sentences 1–3 from exercise 4A. Then match the sentences with descriptions a–c below.

1 I think if he didn't have children, he _____ back home by now.
2 If Skype hadn't been invented, _____ a fortune on phone calls!
3 If some smart person hadn't invented on-demand TV, I _____ my best friend's party!

a past condition with a present result   _____
b past condition with a future result   _____
c present condition with a past result   _____

B Look at three more sentences from exercise 4A. Which words or phrases in **bold** mean *if* and which mean *if not*? Then read the Grammar box.

1 I have to really concentrate when I go somewhere. **Otherwise**, I get lost coming back.
2 Now we never get lost, **as long as** I remember my phone!
3 So I go out in the evenings, **provided** my friends are going out, too.

70

mixed conditionals and alternatives to *if* — LANGUAGE — **8C**

 Grammar | mixed conditionals and alternatives to *if*

Mixed conditionals:
If you **had checked** the map before we left, we **wouldn't be** lost now.
If I **was** a braver person, I **would have chased** the bank robber.
If we **hadn't spent** all our money, we **would be** able to go on vacation this year.
I**'d come** next week if I **hadn't** already **made** plans.

Alternatives to *if / if not*:
If you work hard, you'll pass your exams.
= **As long as** you work hard, you'll pass your exams.
If you **don't** wear a coat, you'll be cold.
= Wear a coat. **Otherwise**, you'll be cold.
If he finishes work on time, he'll make dinner.
= He'll make dinner, **provided** he finishes work on time.

Go to Grammar practice: mixed conditionals and alternatives to *if*, page 109

6 A ▶ 8.11 **Pronunciation: weak forms** Listen to the words *have*, *had*, and *would* in their strong forms and then in their weak forms. Listen again and repeat.

B ▶ 8.12 Listen to the sentences below. Underline the weak forms of the words in **bold**. Listen again and repeat.

1 Provided you **have** read all the instructions, you may begin.
2 If I thought I could help you, I **would** come over.
3 **Had** there been any problems, I **would have** called my uncle.
4 If we **had had** more time, we **would have** stayed for dinner.
5 John **would** be here now if he **hadn't had** an extra class.
6 Jo **wouldn't have** failed the exam if she **had** read the instructions carefully.

7 A Choose the correct options to complete the text.

What if plastic had never been invented?

¹*Had plastic not / Had not plastic* been invented, our water bottles would probably still be glass, and our shopping bags would all be made of paper. You ²*won't have / wouldn't be* reading this on a laptop, and a lot of our clothing and furniture wouldn't even exist. Plastic is strong, lightweight, flexible, and versatile. If it ³*doesn't / didn't* have all these attractive qualities, it ⁴*wouldn't / won't* have become so popular. But despite plastic's many qualities and uses, there's a problem – it's not biodegradable. This makes it one of the worst pollutants on the planet. Some people think that plastic isn't a problem ⁵*supposing / provided* it's recycled, but this misses the point. Ultimately, we must reduce our consumption of plastic. ⁶*Otherwise / Provided*, we will be facing a terrible crisis, particularly in our oceans. As long as we continue to buy plastic goods at our current rate, much of our marine life will become extinct, ⁷*whether / provided* we recycle our plastic or ⁸*not / otherwise*.

B Read the text again. Then, in pairs, complete the sentence below in different ways with past, present, and future results.
If plastic hadn't been invented, …

Go to Communication practice: Student A page 138, Student B page 148

8 Think of some important events in your life. In pairs, discuss the things that would be different in the past, present, and future had those events not happened.

 If you could go back in time and prevent the invention of something, what would it be and why?

71

8 SKILLS WRITING opinion and discussion essays ■ cohesion

8D Role models

1 Discuss the questions in pairs. Give reasons for your answers.
1 Who were your role models when you were growing up?
2 Look at the people in the pictures. What kind of people do you think are the best role models for teenagers nowadays?

2 Read the essay. To what extent does the writer agree with your view of role models?

Who are more appropriate role models for teenagers: people in the public eye or those in a young person's everyday life?

Julie Barton

The teenage years are a very important stage in a person's development, and it is, therefore, crucial that teenagers have appropriate role models. Role models should have a strong moral code, and their achievements should be based on hard work and determination. Traditionally, young people would look up to people in their family and community, but, nowadays, many adolescents look up to people in the public eye. This essay will explain why, in my view, the best role models are people from a young person's everyday life.

Although it is true that some famous people can be positive role models, far too many celebrities set a bad example nowadays. For example, when young people see their favorite athlete cheating, or a famous actor being arrested for aggressive behavior, they could believe that this kind of behavior is acceptable. In addition to **this**, many celebrities nowadays are famous for their wealth and glamour rather than for their achievements in life, which, in my opinion, is not a good example to set, either.

In contrast, a role model from a young person's community represents something more meaningful and permanent. Whether it is a hard-working parent, a neighbor with a strong sense of community, or a teacher with a passion for education, these real-life role models can provide inspiration on a daily basis. Furthermore, due to their actual physical presence, they can communicate with young people face to face and guide them. This personal relationship allows the role model to influence the teenager in an ongoing way.

In summary, it is my view that people in the community make more appropriate role models than people in the public eye, due to their ability to inspire young people in a meaningful way and provide ongoing support. Teenagers should, therefore, be encouraged to establish strong and positive relationships with the people around them, with less value placed on the importance of fame, wealth, and celebrity status.

3 Read the essay again. Are these sentences true (T) or false (F)? Correct the false sentences.
1 Julie first states her general opinion about role models in paragraph 2.
2 Paragraph 2 contains arguments in favor of celebrities as role models.
3 Paragraph 3 contains arguments in favor of people from the local community as role models.
4 Julie acknowledges the opposing viewpoint but only in one sentence, not a paragraph.

opinion and discussion essays ■ cohesion **WRITING** SKILLS **8D**

 Skill opinion and discussion essays

Both opinion essays and discussion essays examine a particular issue or situation. While opinion essays consider one side of the argument and try to persuade the reader of the writer's opinion, discussion essays consider both sides of the argument. They are more balanced and objective.
A common structure for these types of essays is:
1 **Introduction:** gives background information, explains the present situation, and states the writer's argument.
2 **Main body** (two or more paragraphs):
  • **opinion essay** – examines why one side of the argument is correct. The other side of the argument is considered, but it is not given equal weight.
  • **discussion essay** – examines both sides of the argument. Each side of the argument is given equal weight.
3 **Conclusion:** summarizes what the essay has shown and gives recommendations for the future.

4 Read the Skill box and answer the questions.
1 Is Julie's essay an opinion or discussion essay?
2 Does it follow the suggested structure in the Skill box?
3 What background information does Julie give in the introduction?
4 What are Julie's main points in the main body of the essay?
5 What recommendations does she give in the conclusion?

 Text builder cohesion

When we write, it is important that we clearly show the reader the connections between our ideas. This is called *cohesion*. We create cohesion by using:
• **synonyms:** He is *famous* and hangs out with other *well-known* people.
• **reference words** (e.g., pronouns): *The mayor* has always misunderstood *the issue*, and *it* continues to confuse *her*.
• **summary nouns:** Unemployment is at an all-time high. *This situation* …
• **linking words:** *Although* we understand the risks, we want to go ahead with the plan.

5 Read the Text builder. Find the following cohesive devices in Julie's essay and answer the questions.
1 Find two synonyms for "young people" and two synonyms for "people in the public eye" in paragraphs 1 and 2.
2 Look at the word in **bold** in paragraph 2. What does it refer to?
3 Find two summary nouns in paragraph 3. What does each summarize?
4 Find a linking word of reason in paragraph 4. Which ideas does it connect?

6 A Match essay titles a and b with essay extracts 1–4.

a **How successful are schools and colleges at preparing young people for the world of work?**

b **Should educational institutions encourage students to use their phones and tablets in class?**

1 Some people believe that all high-school students should receive career guidance. This is only possible if …
2 There has been a sharp increase in the number of people who own smart devices. This trend …
3 Students should be encouraged to use technology in order to …
4 Children should finish school knowing which career path to follow. An important function of any place of education is …

B Underline the cohesive devices in the essay extracts in exercise 6A. Then complete the sentences with your own ideas.

7 A PREPARE Choose one of the essay titles in exercise 6A. Decide which type of essay you will write (opinion or discussion), and use the Skill box to plan the structure of your essay.
B PRACTICE Write your essay in about 250 words. Use two or three cohesive devices in each paragraph.
C PERSONAL BEST Work in pairs. Read your partner's essay and identify whether it is an opinion or a discussion essay. Is the essay cohesive?

Personal Best Write an introduction to the other essay title in exercise 6A.

73

7 and 8 REVIEW and PRACTICE

Grammar

1 Cross (X) the sentence that is NOT correct.

1. a. My friends advised that I spend less money. ☐
   b. My friends advised I'm spending less money. ☐
   c. My friends advised me to spend less money. ☐
2. a. By 2050, robots will have been doing all the work. ☐
   b. By 2050, robots will be doing all the work. ☐
   c. By 2050, all the jobs will have been taken by robots. ☐
3. a. In my class, there are twenty students, most of whom are from Brazil. ☐
   b. In my class, there are twenty students, some of whom are from Brazil. ☐
   c. In my class, there are twenty students, all of them are from Brazil. ☐
4. a. There's no air-conditioning in the office which I work. ☐
   b. There's no air-conditioning in the office in which I work. ☐
   c. There's no air-conditioning in the office that I work in. ☐
5. a. We wouldn't have gone on vacation if I hadn't saved so much money. ☐
   b. If I hadn't saved so much money, we wouldn't be going on vacation. ☐
   c. We wouldn't be going on vacation if I haven't saved so much money. ☐
6. a. He was going to buy a car the last time I saw him. ☐
   b. He'll have bought a car last time I saw him. ☐
   c. He was buying a car the last time I saw him. ☐

2 Use the words in parentheses to complete the sentences so they mean the same as the first sentence.

1. I've been studying since 7 p.m., and it's almost midnight.
   By midnight _____ for five hours. (studying)
2. "I've been going to a lot of concerts lately," he told me.
   He _____ a lot of concerts lately. (told)
3. Hardly any of the twenty restaurants in this town serve Italian food.
   This city has twenty restaurants, _____ Italian food. (which)
4. The previous manager, who you've heard so much about, resigned last week.
   The previous manager, about _____, resigned last week. (whom)
5. If you've finished your homework, you can watch some TV before you go to bed.
   _____, you can watch some TV before you go to bed. (long)
6. I can't sleep because I had coffee after dinner.
   I'd _____ coffee after dinner. (able)

3 Choose the correct options to complete the text.

Making decisions

I've always hated making decisions. I spend a lot of time regretting the choices I've made and thinking, "If I had done things differently, I would ¹*be / have been being* happier now!" So last June, I started a year-long experiment: every time I had to choose between two options, I would toss a coin and let fate decide. When I explained my plan to my friends, most of ²*them / whom* are very practical people, they all advised me not to ³*do / have done* it. One friend even told me it ⁴*will / would* ruin my life!

It's been a very interesting few months to say the least. ⁵*Had I / I had* not made decisions based on the toss of a coin, I wouldn't have had such different experiences. It has really made my life interesting, but I won't ⁶*have continued / be continuing* with the experiment. ⁷*Supposing / Provided* I have to make a really big decision, can I really let fate decide where I live, what job I do, or who I marry? No. In the future, I'll ⁸*be / have* been making decisions by myself, and who knows? Maybe this time next year, I'll have made a few choices that I don't regret!

Vocabulary

1 Match words and expressions 1–8 with definitions a–h.

1. giveaway _____
2. cursor _____
3. analysis _____
4. mix-up _____
5. worlds apart _____
6. inspire _____
7. classification _____
8. catch-up _____

a. mistake or misunderstanding
b. make someone feel the urge or ability to do something
c. keeping up with someone or something
d. a free gift
e. the arrangement of things into categories
f. very different
g. detailed examination of something
h. the arrow you control on a computer screen

74

REVIEW and PRACTICE — **7 and 8**

2 Complete the sentences with the words in the box.

> influential   fall into place   computer literate
> in the first place   state-of-the-art   proven

1 We believe he is guilty of the crime, but it has not been _____ yet.
2 If you didn't want anyone to know, you shouldn't have told me _____ !
3 If you're not _____ , you'll struggle to get a job.
4 His work has been very _____ . Many scientists have quoted it.
5 The new version of our product features the most recent _____ technology.
6 It's been a difficult few months, but, finally, everything is starting to _____ .

3 Choose the correct options to complete the sentences.

1 Don't forget to *back up / backup* your work before you turn off the laptop.
2 You should have told me the truth *in the first place / in first place*.
3 Watching the Olympics *inspired / innovated* him to become an athlete.
4 I was really looking forward to the party, but it was actually quite a *breakdown / let-down*.
5 The software is very simple to *attach / install*.
6 This is the best restaurant in town. The food is *all over the place / out of this world*.
7 We will need to *evaluate / conclude* your health before we decide on the best therapy.
8 There has been *a breakup / an outbreak* of food poisoning at the hospital.

4 Complete the text with the words in the box.

> wireless network   all over the place   conclusion
> breakup   the end of the world   analyzed   charge

My boyfriend and I were together for three years, but the relationship ended last year. Following the ¹_____ , I was very upset – my feelings were ²_____ . And social media didn't help. It seemed like everyone was having a great time except me! One day I sat down and ³_____ my life. I came to the ⁴_____ that I had to spend some time alone, away from people and social media. So I went camping in the mountains for a couple of weeks. Obviously, there was no ⁵_____ in the mountains, so I couldn't go online, and there was nowhere to ⁶_____ my battery, either. Without those distractions, I had time to think. I realized that although it was sad that the relationship had ended, it wasn't ⁷_____ .

Personal Best

Lesson 7A Think of a conversation when someone has advised you to do something. Write four sentences to report the conversation.

Lesson 7A Name three things you do with a smartphone and three things you do with a computer.

Lesson 7B Write five sentences about possible future events and how likely they are.

Lesson 7C Describe four things that you think will be different in the year 2050.

Lesson 7C Write three sentences with *world* expressions and three sentences with *place* expressions.

Lesson 7D Write two opinions. Then write two sentences to disagree tactfully and introduce an opposite opinion.

Lesson 8A Write four sentences, two about people and two about objects, using relative clauses to give more information.

Lesson 8A Name four things that scientists regularly do, using nouns, adjectives, and verbs.

Lesson 8B Name four nouns that come from phrasal verbs.

Lesson 8C Write three conditional sentences without using *if*.

Lesson 8D Write three sentences with three different cohesive devices.

UNIT 9 Connections

LANGUAGE participle clauses ■ friendship and love

9A Unlikely friendships

1 Look at the statements below. To what extent do you agree with them? Discuss in pairs.

1. A close friend can't be someone you've met recently. To be close, friends have to **go back a long way**.
2. If you don't **hit it off** immediately with someone, you're unlikely to become friends.
3. It's completely normal for friends not to **see eye to eye**. Agreeing about everything would be boring.
4. Some friends just end up **drifting apart**. It's normal, especially if you no longer have anything in common.

Go to Vocabulary practice: friendship and love, page 126

2 A Read the text quickly and answer the questions about the three friendships.

1. In which way is each set of friends "like oil and water"?
2. Why do the friends get along, or why did they drift apart?

Like oil and water

[1]Known to the world as the movie-star clown with the funny glasses, Groucho Marx seemed an unlikely friend for T.S. Eliot, who is regarded as one of the major poets of the twentieth century. However, they admired each other's work, and although their communication was solely through letters, they became close friends. This all changed, though, when they met face to face and found that neither of them was interested in the other's conversation – they quickly realized they were as different as oil and water and didn't stay in touch! But, handled carefully, some unlikely friendships can be more successful. Here are two oil-and-water friendships that have gone the distance.

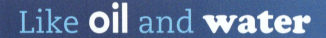

"Marlene and I met on the first day of college. Most people were talking in groups but the woman [2]sitting in the corner looked pretty lonely. [3]Not being shy, I just walked over and introduced myself. I thought she would be pleased, but she looked scared and didn't say a word! I kept trying to make conversation, and, finally, she began talking. I realized that she was just incredibly shy and prefers listening to talking. It's funny because I'm very outgoing, and I like talking to people. I think that's why we get along so well – we really complement each other."

"Jon and I met twelve years ago, so we go back a long way. [4]Having just watched my soccer team lose a game, I heard someone laugh and cheer for the other team. Irritated by his cheering, I started talking to him, and we got along like a house on fire, despite not seeing eye to eye on anything! But I found him funny and honest, and I think that's why our friendship works so well. Although we're honest about our views, meaning we often have arguments, we always make up soon afterward. I mean, life's boring when everyone agrees all the time!"

B Do you know any unlikely friendships? Discuss in pairs.

3 A Match the highlighted phrases in the text (1–4) with the types of participle below.

a present participle _____ _____   b past participle _____   c perfect participle _____

B Match the highlighted participles in the text with the functions a–d. Then read the Grammar box.

a replaces a relative clause to add information about the noun   _____
b describes an action that happened earlier   _____
c adds information about the noun and has a passive meaning   _____
d adds information about the noun and has an active meaning   _____

76

participle clauses ■ friendship and love   **LANGUAGE   9A**

 Grammar participle clauses

Present participles to give extra information:
***Yelling loudly**, I was able to get his attention.*
*Is that your teacher **wearing** the suit and tie?*

Past participles to give extra information:
***Liked** by all her students, Sarah was a fantastic teacher.*
***Driven carefully**, this car should last for 20 years.*

Perfect participles to show a sequence of events:
***Having left** work early, I was home in time for dinner.*

Look! In participle clauses, we can use the *-ing* form with action *and* state verbs (*be*, *know*, *become*, etc.).
***Being** a kind person, she offered to lend me the money.*

Go to Grammar practice: participle clauses, page 110

4 A ▶9.3 **Pronunciation:** intonation in participle clauses Listen to the sentences. Does the intonation go up (↗) or down (↘) at the end of the participle clause?

1 Seeing a large crowd gathering, I walked over to investigate.
2 Holding a newspaper in one hand, she approached my table.
3 Taken twice a day, this medicine should make you feel better soon.
4 Written in 1918, it's one of the nation's favorite poems.
5 Having showered and gotten dressed, I left the house and got in the car.
6 Having studied so hard for the exam, it's such a shame he failed.

B ▶9.3 Listen again and repeat.

Go to Communication practice: Students A and B, page 138

5 ▶9.4 Listen to two people talking about two unlikely relationships. What do you think might be unusual about each relationship?

Selma and Davor

Simon and Gina

6 A Complete the sentences from exercise 5 with participle forms of the verbs in the box. Who says each sentence, Selma or Simon?

be   see   not have   meet   organize   not want   listen   know   sit   introduce

1 _____ any grandparents, I've never really talked to anyone from his generation.
2 _____ by the movie producers, the event is a chance for fans to meet their favorite actors.
3 I was studying in a coffee shop when I saw a man _____ by himself.
4 _____ to upset him, I've never asked his age.
5 _____ a celebrity, she meets a lot of people.
6 For a while, our relationship was a secret _____ only to our closest friends.
7 _____ himself, he began telling me about his life – and it was so interesting!
8 To be honest, _____ her in several movies, I already had a crush on her.
9 I thought she might be a little arrogant, but, _____ her, I realized I was completely wrong.
10 But while _____ to one of his stories about being a young man, I figured out he must be at least 70.

B ▶9.5 Listen and check your answers to exercise 6A.

7 In pairs, describe how you met one of your close friends and what your relationship is like. Use some of the prompts below, or your own ideas.

Being …   Living in …   Having gone to …   Since meeting …   Not wanting to …

Having introduced …   While listening …   Instead of talking …   Before meeting …

Personal Best Write a paragraph about how your parents or grandparents met.

9 SKILLS READING locating specific information ■ reflexive and reciprocal pronouns

9B With a little help from my friends

1 A In pairs, discuss the questions.

1 How many close friends do you think people have on average?
2 What, in your view, are the three main psychological or physical benefits of friendship?

B Read the text quickly and compare the ideas with your answers in exercise 1A.

> **Skill** locating specific information
>
> **Locating specific information in a text is a useful reading skill. It is important to know what type of information you are looking for and where it is likely to be in the text.**
> - Scan each paragraph quickly to get an idea of the topics covered in each section. Topic sentences (the first sentence of each paragraph) often state what the paragraph is about, so read these in more detail.
> - Identify the type of information you are looking for. For example, is it an amount, a place, a reason, an outcome, or a comparison? Look for clues, e.g., currency symbols, capital letters for proper nouns, linkers of reason, etc.
> - Identify the section of the text that is most likely to contain the specific information you need. Scan that section for clues, key words, phrases, and synonyms.

2 A Read the Skill box. Look at the questions below. What kind of information do you need to find? In which paragraph do you think the answer to each question is located?

1 What problem is more common among older people living on their own?
2 Why is it useful to tell your friends about what is worrying you?
3 According to the author, how has the world improved? What has changed for the worse?
4 In what way is losing a friend similar to dental pain?
5 Which groups of people does the author give recommendations to?
6 In one study, what was perceived to be very challenging by one group of participants? What did this show?
7 Which social experiences make us feel as joyful as we would feel if we earned extra amounts of money?
8 Which finding about the physical benefits of friendship does the author find extremely surprising?

B Answer the questions in exercise 2A.

3 Which words are missing in these sentences from the text? Scan the text and check your answers.

1 "I'm really concerned about that exam." "I'm a little nervous _____ , to be honest."
2 Sharing your concerns with _____ is likely to make the situation much less overwhelming.
3 One way to get _____ noticed is to hang out with friends.
4 People who choose to lead a solitary life may be bringing a whole range of psychological and physical problems upon _____ .

> **Text builder** reflexive and reciprocal pronouns
>
> We use reflexive pronouns when the subject and object of the sentence are the same, e.g., *She washed herself.*
> Reflexive pronouns can also be used for other meanings:
> - to emphasize the subject: *Don't worry if you can't tell her. I'll tell her **myself**.*
> - to emphasize there was no help: *I made this dinner **myself**.*
> - "alone": *He spends all day all **by himself**.*
> - "also": *I know you're exhausted. I'm pretty tired **myself**.*
> - "for my use only": *My roommate's away so I have the apartment **all to myself**.*
>
> We use reciprocal pronouns when two people do the same action to the other:
> *They help **each other**.*   *They won't talk to **one another**.*

4 Read the Text builder. Look again at the sentences in exercise 3. Which use of reflexive and reciprocal pronouns is each sentence an example of?

5 Which specific information in the text did you find most interesting or surprising? In pairs, discuss.

78

locating specific information ■ reflexive and reciprocal pronouns   **READING**   SKILLS   9B

Better together:
the benefits of friendship

In many ways, the world has changed, and continues to change, for the better. People are living longer, economies are growing, and global poverty is on the decline. However, in terms of social contact, the trend has generally been downwards. People volunteer less, have fewer children, entertain guests in their home less often, and generally have fewer close friends than previous generations. This is illustrated by a recent sociological study that found that we each have just two close friends, on average, compared to 25 years ago when the average was three.

But why does it matter that social contact is decreasing? The answer, according to scientists, is that having friends is a fundamental human requirement for many different reasons, both psychological and biological. Let's start with a question. Have you ever noticed that problems seem less serious once you've shared them with a friend? "I'm really concerned about that exam," you may say, to which your friend may reply, "I'm a little nervous myself, to be honest." The simple fact of sharing your concerns with each other is likely to make the situation much less overwhelming.

There is research to support this. Students asked by their professor to estimate how steep a hill was judged it differently depending on whether they were with their friends or not. Those whose friends were nearby estimated that the hill was less steep than those standing alone. In other words, simply being close to our friends helps us overcome challenges. And this is just one of the many benefits of friendships and socializing.

Social contact has also been linked to a wide array of different psychological benefits, including higher self-esteem, increased empathy and trust, and generally a higher level of overall happiness. In economic terms, we can equate increases in social contact with the feeling we get when given a pay raise. For example, volunteering once a week leads to an increase in happiness equivalent to that achieved by receiving $55,000 extra a year. Seeing a good friend every day is equivalent to a $100,000 increase in salary. And the benefits are not limited to how we feel about ourselves. If you are looking for romance, one way to get yourself noticed is to hang out with friends, as research suggests we are considered more attractive when in a group than alone.

Physically speaking, people who feel socially connected have better immune systems and may even live longer than those who socialize less. Incredibly, one study even suggested a lack of social contact can be more detrimental to our physical health than a heart condition, while another found that having friends can protect us from various ailments, such as insomnia and exhaustion. Interestingly enough, scientists analyzing brain activity discovered that the ache we feel from the break-up of a relationship is actually not unlike physical pain, such as a toothache. And whereas one pain is telling us to go to the dentist, the other is a message that we should go out and see our friends.

If having friends and socializing benefits both our psychological and physical health, it's unsurprising that a lack of social contact is detrimental. Extreme social isolation in children hinders brain development and leads to a variety of mental, educational, and behavioral problems in later life. At the other end of the age spectrum, isolated elderly people are more likely to suffer from mental deterioration than those with an active social life.

These findings have wide-ranging implications in the areas of work, education, and society in general. On an individual level, people who choose to lead a solitary life may be bringing a whole range of psychological and physical problems upon themselves. Bosses might consider providing social alternatives to financial incentives to their employees. Teachers should encourage collaborative learning, taking advantage of the proven advantages of social contact on the brain's development. And more generally, policy-makers must address the issue of loneliness, since the negative effects, both individually, and on society in general, are significant.

Personal Best   Write an e-mail to a friend summarizing the benefits of friendship in the text above.

9 LANGUAGE

past forms for unreal situations ■ commonly confused words

9C Getting together

1 **A** Read the statement below. What is the difference between the two words in **bold**?

People tend to feel **lonely** when they're **alone**.

B In pairs, discuss to what extent you agree with the statement in exercise 1A.

Go to Vocabulary practice: commonly confused words, page 127

2 Imagine you were asked to suggest a way to help reduce loneliness in your area. What kind of solution would you suggest? Discuss in pairs.

3 **A** Read the text quickly. What three solutions are mentioned? Are they in any way similar to the ones you and your partner came up with in exercise 2?

Alone and lonely? Three great ways to bring people together

The problems associated with loneliness are well known and many people think it's about time we did something about it as a society. Around the world, governments, charities, and individuals are trying different ways to help tackle the issue of social isolation. Here are three of the more innovative suggestions.

What if we began every morning sitting down to talk with the people we shared our block with? That's the idea behind a project called Street Breakfast, which encourages residents to have breakfast outside with each other once a week. Organizer Anthony Gravesen explains the aim of the project. "This is our third Street Breakfast. We know how much people benefit from being on good terms with their neighbors, and we're already seeing new friendships being formed, which is our aim. It's going really well … if only it wasn't raining, though!"

Scientists suggest that singing in groups has a particularly uplifting effect and strengthens our feeling of togetherness. One new member of the Perfect Harmony Choir told us about her experience. "I used to go to soccer games and sing with thousands of people, and it felt amazing. So I thought, what if I joined a choir? I'm so glad I did! Besides the enjoyment of singing in a group, it's just really fun. We all share a common objective that we're working toward – we'll soon be performing at various events around the city. And I've made some great new friends during rehearsals. I just wish I was a better singer."

Many of us would rather our friendships started naturally, by meeting in a class or a club or being introduced by a mutual friend. But, in an increasingly busy world, this has become more difficult. That's where friendship apps come in. You simply create a profile, and the app will find potential friends for you. One user of the app, Xi Jin, is a big fan. "Years ago, dating apps weren't really mainstream, but they've become pretty popular. And I think it's time we saw friendship apps in the same way. Because anything that helps lonely people make friends has to be a good thing."

B Would you recommend the suggestions in the text to anyone you know? Why/Why not?

past forms for unreal situations ■ commonly confused words　LANGUAGE　9C

4 Choose the correct options to complete the sentences. Then check your answers in the text.
1 If only it *isn't / wasn't* raining, though!
2 I just wish I *am / was* a better singer.
3 Many of us would rather our friendships *start / started* naturally.
4 It's time we *see / saw* friendship apps in the same way.

5 A Look at the sentences in exercise 4. Then correct the false information in the rule below.
The speakers use the simple present to talk about unreal present or future situations.

B Look at the sentences below. How are they different from sentences 1 and 2 in exercise 4? Then read the Grammar box.
1 If only it hadn't been raining yesterday!
2 I wish I'd been a better singer when I was younger.

Grammar   past forms for unreal situations

what if / if only:
What if we **walked** instead of driving today?
If only he **didn't live** so far away.
If only he **hadn't moved** so far away.

would rather:
I'd rather you **didn't open** the window.
They'd rather I **stayed** in college.

wish:
Do you wish you **could fly**?
I wish you **weren't leaving** tomorrow.
I wish you **hadn't left** yesterday.

it's (about) time:
It's time the city **improved** services.
It's about time we **left**.

Look! We don't use *It's time* … with negative sentences.
~~It's time we didn't live here any more.~~

Go to Grammar practice: past forms for unreal situations, page 111

6 A ▶9.8　**Pronunciation:** sentence stress　Listen to the sentences and mark the stressed words.
1 What if we left early tomorrow?
2 If only he'd be quiet.
3 I wish I'd taken your advice.
4 It's time we cleaned the apartment.
5 It's about time you grew up!
6 I'd rather you didn't do that.

B ▶9.8　Listen again and repeat.

7 A Complete the mini-conversations with the expressions in the Grammar box and the verbs in parentheses.
1 **A** I _____ (I, make) more of an effort to make friends when I was younger. It's not so easy to make friends in your twenties.
   B Can I give you some advice, or would you _____ (I, listen)?
2 **A** It's about _____ (I, get) to know some new people. Most of my old friends have moved away.
   B You're right. If _____ (you, not be) so shy!
3 **A** I get so bored in the evenings. I _____ (there, be) more things to do around here.
   B What _____ (they, build) a movie theater? That would be fantastic!
4 **A** I'd _____ (everyone, tell) the truth all the time, even if it upset people.
   B Really? I _____ (I, not lie) to you about how great your new haircut was, in that case!
5 **A** I _____ (I, not have) to work tomorrow. I'm exhausted, and I could really do with a day off.
   B Me, too. If _____ (we, can) take a day off whenever we felt like it.

B ▶9.9　Listen and check your answers. In pairs, discuss which of the A sentences are true for you.

Go to Communication practice: Student A page 138, Student B page 148

8 Complete the prompts below with as many ideas as you can. Discuss your sentences in pairs.

| It's time the government … | If only I had … | If only the world wasn't … | It's about time we … |

| I wish my family wouldn't … | I'd rather my friends … | I wish I hadn't … | My parents would rather I … |

Personal Best　Write a short news report about your suggestion in exercise 2.

81

9 SKILLS SPEAKING stating preference ■ supporting your opinions

9D Dilemma

1 What is the most difficult life decision you have ever had to make? What did you decide to do in the end? Discuss in pairs.

2 ▶ 9.10 Watch or listen to the first part of *Talking Zone* and answer the questions.
1. What is Ben's dilemma?
2. What does Abigail think Ben should do?
3. Does Ben make a decision about his dilemma at the end of part one?

3 A Match 1–6 with a–f to make sentences from Ben and Abigail's conversation.
1. No doubt about it,
2. Given the choice,
3. I'd prefer to study something I loved,
4. I'd much rather earn some money
5. I'd just as soon make some money
6. If I were in your shoes,

a. I'd do that, too.
b. than get into debt again.
c. I'd just talk to them about it.
d. rather than work in something I didn't.
e. as wait for a job that might never come.
f. I'd rather do the Masters.

B ▶ 9.10 Watch or listen again and check your answers.

4 Do you agree with Abigail's advice to Ben?

Conversation builder	stating preferences
Stating own preferences	**Stating preferences as advice**
No doubt about it, I'd …	Given the choice, I'd …
I'd prefer to … rather than …	If it were up to me, I'd …
I'd much rather … than …	If I were in your shoes, I'd …
I'd just as soon … as …	If I were you, I'd …
I imagine/guess … would be the best course of action.	Surely, it would be better to …

5 Read the Conversation builder. In pairs, use the expressions to discuss options 1–4. Which would be your preference? Which do you think your partner should do?
1. live in the U.K. / live in the U.S.
2. be invisible / be able to fly
3. have a family at a young age / establish your career and then have a family
4. be given $1 million / be given $20,000 every year for fifty years

6 A ▶ 9.11 Watch or listen to the second part of the show. What does Ben decide to do in the end?

B Do you think he's made the right choice? What would you have done?

7 A Who has these opinions: Ben, Abigail, or Ben's father?
1. Going to college is a waste of time.
2. College isn't a waste of time, despite what older generations might think. Times have changed.
3. There's one thing I know for certain. You can't go through life doing something you don't enjoy.
4. It's pointless starting a degree without having a plan for what to do afterward.
5. You should be very careful combining work and study, as it's overwhelming to do both.
6. I'm fairly sure I can work and study at the same time.

B ▶ 9.11 Watch or listen again and check.

stating preference ■ supporting your opinions   **SPEAKING**   SKILLS   **9D**

8 How do they justify their opinions in exercise 7A? Match opinions 1–6 with justifications a–f.

a Ella dropped out of her program because she took way too much on.
b Neither of my parents went to college, but all my siblings and I did.
c I can do it part time, and a lot of the work is online, so I can fit it around my schedule.
d Did you know that the U.S. has some of the highest college dropout rates in the world?
e By the time I was your age, I'd been running my own business for four years!
f My dad spent the first 20 years of his career in a job he hated, but he changed. He's never been happier.

> **Skill supporting your opinions**
>
> When we state our opinions, we can make them more convincing by offering information that supports our opinions:
> - Give reasons for your opinion, e.g.,
>   *It's just that you can learn so much more in a job than you can in college.*
> - Say how certain you are of your opinion, e.g.,
>   *I'm positive this is the right way forward.*
> - Use facts, examples, or anecdotes to support your opinion, e.g.,
>   *By the time I finished college, Anjelica had been managing a store for two years!*

9 Jen and Carla are talking about learning Mandarin. Order sentences a–h to make a conversation.

a ☐ **Jen** I'm not so sure about that. Remember how homesick Vera got when she went to Chile?
b ☐ **Carla** It doesn't have to be. My aunt's friend lives in Shanghai, and she has a spare room. I'm pretty sure she'd put you up for a month or two.
c [1] **Jen** Did I tell you I'm thinking of starting classes at the Orchid school?
d ☐ **Carla** I just think you're more likely to improve that way. And it will be an amazing experience!
e ☐ **Jen** I'm sure that's true, but living abroad can be so expensive and difficult to arrange.
f ☐ **Carla** To learn how to speak Mandarin? That's great, but surely it would be better to go to China?
g ☐ **Jen** I didn't know that! Wow, that would be great! So, you definitely think I should do that then?
h ☐ **Carla** But you're much more adventurous than she is. Besides, I read an article saying the best way to learn a language is to immerse yourself in it.

Go to Communication practice: Students A and B, page 139

10 A PREPARE Work with a partner. Choose a dilemma below. Think how you could explain your dilemma, and state your preference to a friend. How will you support your opinions?

> You changed cities for a job. The job's going well, but you have no social life or work-life balance. You're thinking of resigning so you can move back to your city, even though there aren't many jobs available.

> You've been studying in a three-year professional program for a year. The problem is that you have no money, and no time to see friends or have any outside interests. You're thinking of dropping out.

B PRACTICE Take turns explaining your dilemma and stating your preference. As you listen to your partner's dilemma, give him/her advice. In both cases, try to make a decision.

C PERSONAL BEST Did you say what you'd prefer to do and support your opinions with examples, facts, and anecdotes? Exchange situations and repeat the Practice stage with another partner.

Personal Best Write a short conversation between you and a friend about a dilemma.

UNIT 10
Being human

LANGUAGE distancing language ■ humans and self

10A Humans vs. animals

1 Read the statements. What do the words in **bold** mean? Do you agree with the statements?
1 Both **human beings** and animals have a sense of **self**.
2 Unlike humans, animals are incapable of **selfless** behavior.
3 **Humankind** can share information, which is our biggest advantage over the animal kingdom.

Go to Vocabulary practice: humans and self, page 128

2 A Read the text and check your answers to exercise 1.

Humans vs. animals: what makes us special?

As human beings, we tend to believe that we are superior to all other species. But animals display behavior that seems to suggest that humankind is not as special as we think. Apparently, whales are grateful when they are freed from fishing lines, and it is believed that elephants show sympathy when caring for injured members of the herd. And although for many years, human beings were thought to be the only species to understand fairness, recent studies suggest this is not the case, with both monkeys and rats refusing food if they think another animal will be hurt.

Not only can animals display selfless behavior, but it seems they also have a sense of self. Experiments show that some animals recognize their own image in a mirror. And although it is believed that animals are incapable of planning, there is a chimpanzee in a Swedish zoo that gathers a pile of stones every morning, seemingly so he can throw them at visitors later that day! And the surprises don't stop there. Not only do animals use tools, there is reported to be a species of bird that uses its beak to make tools. If behaviors that we had previously considered uniquely human are being observed in animals, it begs the question: what makes us special?

It would appear that our ability to share knowledge and information sets us apart from other species. Animals can pass on knowledge through demonstration, but humans are capable of using symbolic language to express complex ideas. We can talk about the past, the future, and imaginary situations, and even communicate these across the world. Furthermore, our shared knowledge has been acquired over thousands of years, thanks to our ability to write information down. In this way, humankind seems to have been constantly developing the equivalent of an enormous communal brain, something that animals are unlikely to be able to do, ever.

B Read the text again. Find three abilities that only humans have, and three human-like behaviors that animals display. Which piece of information did you find the most interesting?

3 Match the two parts of the sentences to make complete sentences from the text.
1 **Apparently**, whales are
2 **It is believed that** elephants show
3 Human beings **were thought to** be
4 **There is reported to** be a species of bird that uses
5 **It would appear that** our ability to share
6 Humankind **seems to** have been constantly developing

a knowledge and information sets us apart from other species.
b sympathy when caring for injured members of the herd.
c grateful when they are freed from fishing lines.
d the equivalent of an enormous communal brain.
e its beak to make tools.
f the only species to understand fairness.

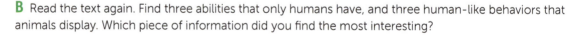

distancing language ■ humans and self **LANGUAGE 10A**

4 Look at the sentences in exercise 3. Why did the author of the text use the words in **bold**? Read the Grammar box.

a to say that he/she is certain the information in the sentence is true
b to avoid saying that the information is definitely true

Grammar — distancing language

Passive structures:
He **is thought to** be the oldest man in the world.
He **is said to** be surprised by the news.
It has been reported that 100 jobs will be lost.

appear/seem:
It appears that the bus was exceeding the speed limit.
There seems to be a problem with your order.
It would seem/appear that the president lied.

Distancing expressions:
Apparently, the neighbors are moving.
According to Sam, the lecture has been canceled.

Look! We use the perfect infinitive to talk about the past:
He is said **to have been** surprised by the news.   There seems **to have been** a problem with your order.

Go to Grammar practice: distancing language, page 112

5 A ▶ 10.4 **Pronunciation:** emphasizing uncertainty Listen to the sentences. Which words are stressed in order to emphasize uncertainty?

1 Apparently, taxes are going up again this year.
2 Excuse me? There seems to be a problem with my check.
3 It appears to have been raining, but it's stopped now.
4 The minister is thought to have resigned, but we're not sure.
5 There are said to be over six thousand languages in the world.
6 According to the president, the journalists are lying.

B ▶ 10.4 Listen again and repeat.

6 A Read the information about humans and animals below. In pairs, make sentences using the words in parentheses to distance yourself from the information. In some sentences, more than one solution is possible.

1 Birds can see colors that humans can't. (thought)
2 Some lizards can run on water. (appear)
3 Humans don't have the biggest brains in the animal kingdom. (apparently)
4 Humans are the only species that write things down. (seems)
5 Humans are not the only animal to fight wars. (according / scientists)
6 Birds can predict storms. (believed)
7 Selflessness is common among children. (seems)
8 Humans know what other humans are thinking, just by looking at their faces. (appear)

B Which piece of information do you find the most surprising?

Go to Communication practice: Student A page 139, Student B page 148

7 A In pairs, look at the pictures and consider the statement below. Think of arguments in favor of the statement, using information from this lesson and your own ideas.

"Animal rights should be as important as human rights."

B Debate the statement with your partner.

Personal Best Write a paragraph about information you've heard about your local area.

85

10 **SKILLS** **LISTENING** understanding numbers ■ final /t/ and /d/ sounds ■ verbs with *re-, over-, mis-*

10B Breaking boundaries

1 What three achievements in your life so far are you proudest of? Discuss in pairs.

2 Complete the sentences about personal achievements with the verbs in the box.

> misinterpret   misunderstand   overcome   recreate

1 I'd like to _____ my fear of water by learning to swim.
2 I want to learn to read maps properly so that I don't _____ them and get lost when I'm hiking.
3 I learned to cook so I could _____ some of the amazing food I've seen on TV.
4 I want to become fluent in German so that I don't _____ my German mother-in-law!

Go to Vocabulary practice: verbs with *re-, over-, mis-*, page 129

3 10.7 Watch or listen to the first part of *Talking Zone*. Choose the correct option to complete the sentences.

1 Sara, Cathy, and Rich all talk about *what they'd like to achieve in life / their most valued achievements*.
2 Kerry-Anne's podcast is about boundaries broken in various *types of sports / areas of life*.
3 Her survey is about the greatest things humanity *has ever done / has done in the last century*.
4 The majority of suggestions were for *scientific / technological* achievements.

🔧 **Skill** understanding precise and imprecise numbers

When listening for detailed information, we often need to understand information that contains numbers. This information can be expressed both precisely and imprecisely.

- Listen for phrases that express a precise number, limit, proportion, or comparison, e.g., *exactly six, in no more than 1,200 words, three out of every five people, three times as many people*
- Recognize decimals, fractions, and percentages, e.g., *9.58 nine point five eight, ¾ three-quarters, 15.05% fifteen point oh five percent*
- Listen for phrases that express an imprecise number, e.g., *somewhere in the region of a dozen, roughly a quarter, five, give or take a few, just under/over an hour, an estimated 20 people*

4 ▶ 10.7 Read the Skill box. Then watch or listen again. Complete the text with phrases and numbers.

You voted: greatest human achievements

[1]_____ of all suggestions were for technological achievements. Of those, [2]_____ of people voted for smartphones, and [3]_____ suggested the invention of the Internet. But [4]_____ people voted for the moon landing.

In science, [5]_____ people voted for the discovery of gravity and roughly the same amount – [6]_____ – suggested penicillin. But [7]_____ of the votes were for the discovery of DNA's helix structure.

In sports, a lot of people voted for Simone Biles' Olympic performances in gymnastics, and [8]_____ voted for Michael Phelps' [9]_____ gold medals. But [10]_____ voted for Usain Bolt's record-breaking [11]_____ second 100 m. sprint.

understanding numbers ■ final /t/ and /d/ sounds ■ verbs with *re-*, *over-*, *mis-*   **LISTENING**   SKILLS   **10B**

5 Discuss the questions in pairs.
1 Do you agree with the most popular suggestions in each category in exercise 4?
2 Which greatest human achievements would you have suggested? Why?

6 ▶ 10.8 Watch or listen to the second part of the show. Answer the questions.
1 What limit do scientists think we have almost reached in sports?
2 In which area are there still many boundaries to be broken?
3 Kerry-Anne mentions three specific boundaries still to be broken. What are they?

7 ▶ 10.8 Watch or listen again. Are the sentences true (T) or false (F)? Correct the false sentences.
1 There is very little evidence to show that humans are close to reaching our physical limits.
2 There is a limit to how fast horses can run, and this also appears to be true for humans.
3 The current record for the women's 100-meter race is 10 seconds.
4 In 100 years, ice skaters have gone from rotating once to roughly four times in a jump.
5 NASA isn't interested in sending people to Mars in the next few decades.
6 It is believed that cars will be able to fly in the near future.
7 "Mind-uploading" is the only technique being studied for breaking the boundary of mortality.
8 Our motivations for breaking boundaries today are the same as those of our ancestors.

Listening builder   final /t/ and /d/ sounds

When a word ends in a /t/ or a /d/ sound, and the next word begins with a consonant, the /t/ and /d/ sounds are often dropped.
The /t/ and /d/ sound in frequently used "grammar" words, e.g., *and*, *but*, *that*, is often dropped. This can happen even when the next word begins with a vowel sound.
You spoke abou(t) the fac(t) tha(t) we coul(d) be nearing the limit of boundary breaking.
There is an opinion, which is hel(d) by many doctors an(d) scientists, tha(t) we are close to reaching those limits.

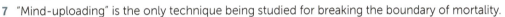

8 ▶ 10.9 Read the Listening builder. Listen and complete the sentences with up to four words in each blank.
1 Apparently, we are starting to reach our physical limits in things like gymnastics _____ field.
2 A _____ horse racing and _____ was a limit to how fast horses _____ .
3 Sending people to Mars is _____ be a boundary worth breaking. All in all, I think there's a _____ we'll _____ soon.
4 Lots of _____ are looking into this, _____ first flying cars are only a few years away.
5 Many scientists are looking into immortality, _____ are lots of ways this _____ achieved.

9 Discuss the questions in pairs.
1 What do you think of the current technological developments mentioned in the show? Is your attitude about them positive or negative? Explain why.
2 In which fields do you think humanity's next great achievements will occur? What do you think those achievements will be?
3 Which boundaries would you like to see broken in your lifetime? Why?
4 Are there any boundaries that you think will be impossible to break?
5 What do you hope to achieve in your lifetime?

Personal Best   Write a paragraph about an amazing human achievement. Include some facts and figures.

10 LANGUAGE — adverbs and adverbial phrases ■ adverb collocations

10C Faith in humanity

1 What's the nicest thing the following people have done for you? Discuss in pairs.

1 a friend   2 a relative   3 a teacher or lecturer   4 a stranger

2 A Read the headline of the article below and look at the pictures. What do you think the stories are about?

B Read the stories and check your answers to exercise 2A.

GOOD NEWS: stories to restore your faith in humanity

Nowadays, most news headlines and stories are full of doom and gloom. Here we present our favorite good news stories from around the world.

In 2016, Jeni Stepien was planning her wedding, but was upset that her father wouldn't be walking her down the aisle. Sadly, he had died ten years earlier, and his heart had been donated to another man, Arthur Thomas. However, Jeni had the fantastic idea of inviting Arthur and asked him to walk her down the aisle on her special day. Arthur was deeply touched by Jeni's request and agreed. At the ceremony, Jeni pressed her hand hard against Arthur's chest and, feeling the beat of her father's heart, told all the guests that the whole family was there. Jeni and Arthur remain close, and they speak on the phone as often as they can.

This is five-year-old Murtaza Ahmadi from Afghanistan proudly wearing a plastic bag with blue-and-white stripes, similar to the soccer shirt of Argentina's national team. On his back is the name of his favorite soccer player, Lionel Messi. The photo went viral, and, as a result, was seen by millions, including Messi himself. The Barcelona forward was highly impressed by the improvised shirt, so much so that he sent Murtaza a real signed one. Unsurprisingly, the little boy was utterly delighted, and things got even better when he was invited onto the field with Messi at a game in Qatar. He looked like he could hardly believe what was happening!

In 2016, Dion Leonard went to China to run the grueling 250 km. Gobi Desert March. Halfway through the race, a stray dog appeared from nowhere and ran alongside Dion for more than 100 km. – an utterly extraordinary feat! Dion decided to adopt the dog, who he named Gobi, and take her home with him to Scotland. Soon after he made the decision, however, Gobi disappeared. It seemed highly unlikely that she would ever be found alive, but Dion strongly believed she would survive and organized a team of volunteers to find her. Eventually, she was found, and Dion took her home to Scotland.

3 In pairs, answer the questions.

1 Which story restores your faith in humanity the most?
2 Which other good news stories have you heard recently?

4 A Look at the underlined adverbial phrases in the article. Write them in the chart in the correct row. Do they come at the beginning, in the middle, or at the end of a clause?

Type of adverb	Example	Position
time		
place		
manner		
frequency		
comment		

adverbs and adverbial phrases ■ adverb collocations   LANGUAGE **10C**

B Look at the highlighted words in the article. Choose the correct option to complete the rules. Then read the Grammar box.

1 Use *deeply / utterly* with extreme adjectives.
2 Use *deeply / highly* with feelings and emotions.
3 Use *strongly / highly* with positive words and probability.
4 *hard* and *hardly* have *the same / a different* meaning.

Go to **Vocabulary practice:** adverb collocations, page 129

Grammar — adverbs and adverbial phrases

Common adverb collocations:
It was **utterly astonishing**.
We **strongly oppose** this decision.
I'm **deeply ashamed** of what I did.
It's **highly probable** he will resign.

Adverb position:
Amazingly, I got to work on time despite the traffic.
She **very rarely** comes here any more.
I didn't realize my mistake **at the time**.

Adverbs with two forms:
Hold **tight** or you'll fall. Grip the knife **tightly**. (= similar meaning)
I work **hard**. I've **hardly** seen you today! (= different meaning)

Look! When there is more than one type of adverb in the end position, the typical order is manner, place, time.
I've been working **hard in the library all morning**.

Go to **Grammar practice:** adverbs and adverbial phrases, page 113

5 A ▶ 10.12 **Pronunciation:** word stress Listen to the sentences below. Underline the stressed syllables in the words in **bold**. Listen again and repeat.
1 I think that taking Gobi to a different country is **potentially** damaging to her health.
2 I'm not surprised he came to her wedding. Humans are **naturally** kind and helpful.
3 I **sincerely** hope that Messi stayed in touch with the boy.
4 Running 250 km. is **undoubtedly** impressive, but it's also **utterly** pointless.
5 **Presumably**, Mr. Thomas was already in touch with Jeni before she asked him.

B Do you agree with the statements in exercise 5A? Discuss them with your partner.

6 ▶ 10.13 Listen to six short conversations. Then use a word from each box below to complete the sentences about each situation.

bitterly heavily severely incredibly potentially downright	expensive criticized rude fatal disappointed damaged

1 The car is _____ and can't be driven.
2 The cost of the soccer player's transfer is _____ .
3 The person could have had a _____ accident.
4 The store manager and salesclerk were _____ .
5 The mayor's plans have been _____ .
6 The concert was awful, and the friends were _____ .

Go to **Communication practice:** Student A page 140, Student B page 149

7 In pairs, tell your partner about:

- a time you were utterly exhausted.
- a time you were looking forward to something, but ended up bitterly disappointed.
- the last time you struggled to do something, but eventually managed to do it.
- a time you had to get up ridiculously early.
- a person or experience that was downright unpleasant.
- a book or movie that was heavily criticized.
- something you strongly believe in, and something you absolutely disagree with.

Write a short news report about a good news story.

89

10 SKILLS WRITING summarizing data ■ cautious language

10D A growing trend

1 A Look at the chart below. From 2004 to 2015, did ownership rates of each device:
  a increase?
  b decrease?
  c increase and then decrease?
  d stay at a similar rate?

B Which trend do you find most surprising? In pairs, discuss the possible reasons for the different trends.

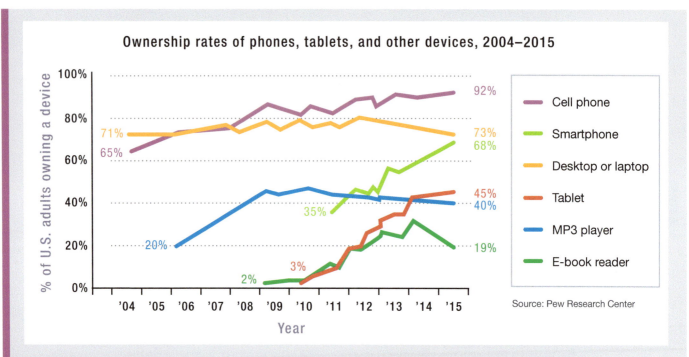

This chart shows the changing ownership rates in the U.S. of six different technological devices between 2004 and 2015. Perhaps the first trend to notice is that ¹there is a lot of variation between the changes in ownership rates of the different devices.

Although there was an increase in ownership of both cell phones in general and smartphones in particular, the rates of increase are very different. Whereas ownership of cell phones ²rose steadily over 10 years, ownership of smartphones almost doubled in 4 years. This is presumably because most people already owned a cell phone, while smartphones were a relatively new invention in 2011.

³In a similar trend, ownership of laptop and desktop computers remained at a steady rate, but there was a sharp increase in tablet ownership. A possible explanation for this is that as more people own tablets, they no longer need traditional computers.

Another interesting trend concerns the data for MP3 players and e-book readers, both of which showed increased growth for a few years, but then ownership rates began to drop. In particular, ownership of e-book readers suddenly fell from 32% in 2014 to just 19% a year later. These trends are probably also due to the increase in multipurpose smartphones and tablets, which tend to incorporate music players and document readers.

In conclusion, it seems likely that as smartphones become increasingly multipurpose, separate technological devices will become unnecessary and, therefore, rates of ownership will continue to drop.

2 A Read the summary of the data. Underline one trend in each paragraph. Which trend does the writer suggest is the most significant?

B What explanations are given for the observed trends in phone, computer, and other device ownership?

3 Match highlighted phrases 1–3 in the text with functions a–c.
  a to describe change ____
  b to highlight similarities ____
  c to highlight differences ____

summarizing data ■ cautious language **WRITING** **SKILLS** **10D**

 Skill summarizing data

When summarizing data presented in a chart:
- familiarize yourself with the title, labels, and key on the chart.
- identify the main trends that the data shows. These could be increases, decreases, rates of change, similarities, and differences.
- think of possible explanations for the trends you have identified.
- when describing change, use a variety of expressions for different types of changes, e.g., *rose steadily, fell dramatically, a slight increase, a substantial drop.*
- use signposting to help the reader navigate your writing, e.g., *It can clearly be seen that …, The most significant change is …, In contrast to X … .*

4 Read the Skill box. Circle examples of language which describe change in the text. Underline examples of signposting language.

5 Look at the text again. What is the purpose of the word *presumably* in paragraph 2?

 Text builder cautious language

We use cautious language when we are writing, especially in academic contexts. This helps us avoid expressing absolute certainty and avoid overgeneralizations. We can do this by using:
- modals and other verbs: *can, could, may, might, should, (would) seem, (would) appear, tend.*
- probability adjectives and adverbs: *likely, possible, probable, possibly, probably, perhaps, presumably.*
- quantifiers and frequency adverbs: *most, some, the majority, certain types of, sometimes, frequently, generally.*

6 Read the Text builder. Find examples of cautious language in the summary of the data.

7 Use the words in parentheses to make these sentences more cautious.
1 The most important global trend is the increase in income inequality. (perhaps)
2 The rise in global temperatures is caused by humans. (appear)
3 People live for longer now because their diets are healthier. (generally, partly)
4 Graduates get better jobs than people who don't go to college. (majority)
5 Schools will start closing because of the rise of online learning. (could)
6 Increased immigration will lead to more competition at work. (likely)

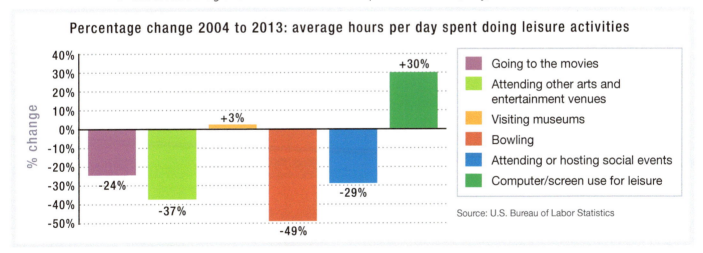

8 A **PREPARE** With a partner, identify the main trends shown in the chart above. Discuss possible explanations for these. Plan a structure for a summary of the data.

B **PRACTICE** Use the Skill box to help you write the summary. Use cautious language when reporting the data and when giving possible explanations for the trends.

C **PERSONAL BEST** Work in pairs. Read your partner's summary and correct any mistakes. What do you like best about the essay? How could you improve it?

Personal Best Write a paragraph about a growing trend in your generation.

9 and 10 REVIEW and PRACTICE

Grammar

1 Check (✓) the correct sentences.

1 a The election is appeared to have been very close. ☐
  b The election is believed to have been very closely. ☐
  c The election is thought to have been very close. ☐
2 a Mildly irritated, I left without ordering. ☐
  b Widely irritated, I left without ordering. ☐
  c Vaguely irritating, I left without ordering. ☐
3 a I wish you hadn't this morning answered the phone! ☐
  b I'd rather you won't answer the phone this morning! ☐
  c If only you hadn't answered the phone this morning! ☐
4 a Henry is strongly disappointed according to my sister. ☐
  b According to my sister, Henry is bitterly disappointed. ☐
  c Henry is strongly disappointed according my sister. ☐
5 a My neighbor seems to be quite strange. ☐
  b My neighbor appears be quite strange. ☐
  c My neighbor is appearing quite strange. ☐
6 a It's time the city starts fixing the roads around here. ☐
  b It's time around here the city started fixing the roads. ☐
  c It's about time the city started fixing the roads around here. ☐

2 Use the words in parentheses to complete the sentences so they mean the same as the first sentence.

1 I worked hard all year, so I felt confident about the exam.
   _____ , I felt confident about the exam. (having)
2 She doesn't want you to call her by her first name.
   She _____ call her by her first name. (rather)
3 We think the government will announce details of the plans next week.
   The government _____ details of the plans next week. (expected)
4 Because he wasn't used to meeting new people, he seemed nervous.
   _____ new people, he seemed nervous. (being)
5 I regret not bringing my ID.
   _____ my ID! (only)
6 We think there were some mistakes in the article.
   _____ some mistakes in the article. (seems)

3 Choose the correct options to complete the text.

Dinner for one?

While [1]sat / sitting alone at my desk yesterday morning, [2]eating / eaten a ready-made sandwich, I read a very interesting article about eating habits. [3]Apparently, / According to recent research [4]suggests / appears that eating together makes us happy. Although this news is [5]hard / hardly surprising, and the benefits of spending time with others are [6]highly / widely known, it is how important it is that I found astonishing. Incredibly, eating alone [7]shows / is shown to be the biggest single factor for unhappiness, besides mental illness. The findings start to become [8]deeply / strongly concerning for society when, [9]according / appearing to a recent survey, we eat almost 50% of our meals alone. So what can we do? Many of us wish we [10]could / can share our mealtimes with friends and family, but it simply isn't possible. My suggestion is to reach out to strangers. We often see other people [11]having / had lunch alone – [12]if only / what if we simply asked to join them?

Vocabulary

1 Put the words in the box in the correct columns.

inhumane   benefit   self-centered   self-conscious
mistreat   rejuvenate   complement   lonely
get along like a house on fire   hit it off
have someone's back   selfless

Positive connotations	Negative connotations

92

REVIEW and PRACTICE 9 and 10

2 Complete the opposite words and expressions.
1 insult – c____t
2 become close – d____ a____
3 disagree – s____e____t____e____
4 former – l____r
5 with other people – a____e
6 disadvantage – b____t
7 in-company staff – s____-e____d
8 in motion – s____y

3 Choose the correct options to complete the sentences.
1 His brother works for a charity which does a lot of *humane / humanitarian* work around the world.
2 What is the greatest obstacle you have had to *overcome / overcharge* in your life?
3 My sister *dates / has a crush* on her neighbor, but he doesn't seem to realize!
4 I'm a little worried about your *self-discipline / self-esteem* because you don't seem very confident right now.
5 We won't be able to come on Saturday because we already have a *commitment / compromise*.
6 I made a complaint to the store when I realized I'd been *overcharged / recharged*.
7 We tried to *recharge / recreate* our first evening together, but it just wasn't the same.
8 Having been together for six years, we decided it was time to *settle down / go back a long way*.
9 You're not being very *rational / rationale*. And *beside / besides*, we've already had this discussion.
10 My brother is overly shy and *self-conscious / self-centered*. He hates going to parties.

4 Complete the text with the words in the box.

bonded   recharge   human nature   overheard
self-employed   rational   alone   overcome

I'm a designer, and I'd just finished a difficult project. I was tired and stressed, and I needed to ¹_____ my batteries, so I went on vacation to Italy. Because I'm ²_____ , I can go on vacation when I like. One evening, I was sitting ³_____ in a restaurant listening to people talking at the table next to me – it's just ⁴_____ to listen to other people's conversations! Anyway, I ⁵_____ someone talking about the project I'd just been working on! It turns out she was someone I'd been sending regular e-mails to for months! We talked about the project and all the challenges we had ⁶_____ , and we ⁷_____ by gossiping about our colleagues! The ⁸_____ part of my brain says our meeting was just a coincidence, but I like to think it was fate.

Personal Best

Lesson 9A Describe something that happened to you, using two present and two past participle clauses.

Lesson 9A Describe a past relationship between two people you know, using expressions of friendship and love.

Lesson 9B Write three sentences about the benefits of friendship using reflexive and reciprocal pronouns.

Lesson 9C Describe two things you regret and two things you think should happen now, using past tenses for unreal situations.

Lesson 9C Name four pairs of commonly confused words and describe the difference between them.

Lesson 9D Write a short conversation where you state a preference on a topic you feel strongly about.

Lesson 10A Describe three things you have read or heard, using distancing language.

Lesson 10A Write four sentences that include two *human* words and two *self* words.

Lesson 10B Name one word with a *re-* prefix, one word with a *mis-* prefix and one word with an *over-* prefix. Use the words in three sentences.

Lesson 10C Name five common adverb collocations and write sentences with three of them.

Lesson 10D Write three sentences on a serious topic you're not totally sure about, using cautious language.

93

GRAMMAR PRACTICE

6A The passive

 6.4

The thief finally **got caught** last week and **got sent** to prison.
This building **has been renovated** twice since it **was built**.
I've just **gotten** my hair **cut** in a totally new style.
Could I **have** the package **delivered**, please?
I'**m** not **used to being told** what to do!
Amy never **expected to be chosen** for the team.

get vs. *be* passive

We can form the passive with *get* or *be*. We use the *get* passive in more informal situations. It is only used with action verbs.

Can you believe it? I got fined for parking here! = I was fined for parking here.
Great news. I might get hired at the local library. = I might be hired at the local library.

Some common verbs used with the *get* passive include *accept*, *catch*, *choose*, *elect*, *fire*, *hire*, *injure*, *kill*, *lay off*, *pay*, *promote*, *rob*, *search*, and *suspend*.

I can't believe he got elected president!
Three of us got fired last month.

We use the *be* passive in most other situations. It can be used with verbs that express states.

The new mayor was disliked by everyone. NOT ~~got disliked~~
Henry was needed at home, so he had to go. NOT ~~got needed~~

It can also be used in formal speech and writing.

The suspects were arrested at 9:30 p.m. and promptly taken to the courthouse.
The documents have been delivered to the attorney's office.

get vs. *have* causative

We use the causative to say that we have arranged for someone to do something for us. It can also be used when someone does something to us. The *get* causative is more informal than the *have* causative.

We got our windows cleaned. = We had our windows cleaned.
I'll get this top dry-cleaned. = I'll have this top dry-cleaned.
Bill got his suitcase stolen. = Bill had his suitcase stolen.

With *-ing* forms

We form *-ing* passives with *being* + a past participle. We usually use the *-ing* form as the subject of a sentence, with verbs such as *enjoy*, *mind*, *miss*, and *prefer*, and after a direct object or a preposition.

Being admitted to this college changed my life!
Do you worry about being criticized by your boss?
I miss being taken care of by my family.
I'm excited about you being considered for this competition!

With infinitives

We form passive infinitives with *to be* + a past participle. We usually use passive sentences with infinitives after adjectives, with verbs such as *expect*, *forget*, *hope* and *need*, and to give a reason.

I'm likely to be called back for a second interview.
I hope to be sent to the conference in New York.
I'm waiting to be connected to the finance department.

1 Complete the sentences using the correct form of the verbs in parentheses.

1 I have no idea who this building _____ by, but I think it dates from 1879. (be, design)
2 The police are confident that the robbers _____ soon. (get, catch)
3 I think I need a new computer. Mine _____ already _____ twice this month. (be, fix)
4 This rental car is so dirty! It doesn't _____ very often, I don't think. (get, wash)
5 When Martha _____ her purse _____ , she was very upset. (get, steal)
6 A new bridge _____ currently, so hopefully the traffic in this neighborhood will improve. (be, build)

2 Complete the second sentences so they have the same meaning as the first sentences. Use the verb in parentheses.

1 The company laid Mary off last month. (get)
   Mary _____
2 Jeff's car has been fixed by a mechanic. (have)
   Jeff _____
3 Someone will rob us unless we get an alarm. (get)
   We _____
4 I should really ask my eye doctor to test my eyes. (get)
   I _____
5 I'll ask someone to wrap this for you. (have)
   I _____

3 Complete the sentences with the correct *be* passive form of the verbs in the box.

| ask | call | interrupt | promote | teach | replace |

1 This is the third time the neighbor's kids have broken my window. They need _____ a lesson!
2 These computers are outdated and are likely _____ soon.
3 My presentation didn't go as planned because I kept _____ all the way through.
4 Bob expects _____ to senior manager next year.
5 _____ how old I am annoys me.
6 My cousin insists on _____ Bartholomew. He says he hates "Bart."

◀ Go back to page 49

6C Using linkers

6.10

The concert was canceled **due to the fact that** the singer was sick.
We'd better leave now **or** we may miss our flight.
We had to raise more money. **Consequently**, we decided to try crowdfunding.
I sent my application immediately **so as to** be sure to be accepted.
I still can't play tennis **in spite of** the fact that I've taken lessons.
Unlike many people I know, I love living with my parents.

Reason
We use the linkers *because*, *as*, and *since* to express a reason.
Since I only read e-books, I've thrown out many of my paper books.
Before a noun, we use *due to*, *because of*, and *owing to*. When *due to* is followed by a clause, we use *due to the fact that*.
Due to/Because of/As a result of sickness, we had to cancel the concert.
The library closed due to the fact that it had no money. NOT *due to it had no money*

Result
We can use *so* or *or* to express the result or consequence of an action.
We left home too late, so we missed our flight.
Don't text at the table or I'll take away your phone.
We can also use *as a result*, *therefore*, and *consequently*. They are more formal.
There are too many cars on the road. Consequently, pollution has increased.

Purpose
We can use *(in order) to*, *(in order) not to*, and *so (that)* to express a purpose.
I decided to invite Nick in order not to seem rude.
We can also use *so as (not) to*, which is a little more formal.
She studied extra hard so as to improve her grades.

Contrast and comparison
We can use *although*, *even though*, *though*, *however*, *nevertheless*, *in spite of*, *despite*, *whereas*, *while*, and *unlike* to express contrast and comparison. *Although*, *even though*, and *though* have the same meaning. *Although* is more formal.
Even though/Although I hate studying, I have to do it every evening.
I hated my apartment. I loved the neighborhood, though.
However and *nevertheless* mean *but*, but are a little more formal.
I didn't do well in high school. Nevertheless/However, I went on to get a Ph.D.
In spite of and *despite* are often followed by a noun or the *-ing* form of a verb. After a clause, we use *the fact that*.
Despite taking singing lessons, I've never learned to sing in tune.
In spite of/Despite the fact that I hate large crowds, I went out on New Year's Eve.
Whereas and *while* express contrast. We can also use *unlike*.
Most older people still watch TV, while younger people watch online.
Unlike most people I know, I hate shopping.

Look! *Therefore*, *consequently*, *as a result*, *however*, and *nevertheless* can't be preceded by a comma. Start a new sentence or use a semicolon.
There's little money in the budget; consequently, we can't hire new staff.
I don't have the money for a vacation. However, I'll probably take one anyway.

GRAMMAR PRACTICE

1 Complete the text with the words in the box.

although	as	due to	however
in order to	or	so	therefore

Have you ever considered funding a project on a crowdfunding platform? If so, ask yourself these important questions:

1 Is it too good to be true?
Trust your instincts ¹_____ you might get into trouble. New developers sometimes lack technical expertise. ²_____ , they may come up with ideas that just aren't feasible. Other "inventors" may sound great. ³_____ , they have no intention of ever launching their product. They start campaigns ⁴_____ make money, and then disappear!

2 Who are the people behind the product?
⁵_____ Kickstarter and Indiegogo have profile pages for new developers, you can learn more about them. And be sure to Google their names, as well, ⁶_____ you can read about their background. Some projects fail ⁷_____ poor planning, which means that experience is important.

3 When should I buy it?
Finally, ⁸_____ it can be exciting to be the first person to own something you've helped create, it's really better to wait until it reaches the general market. That way, you'll know any problems have been corrected.

2 Check (✓) the sentences if they are correct, or correct any mistakes. Remember to check the punctuation.
1 Unlike most people in the office, I go to work by car.
2 As a result it was raining, the game was canceled.
3 Tom made a lot of mistakes due to he didn't have enough experience.
4 I think Rosario is Mexican. I'm not sure, though.
5 Lucy won the game despite she was injured.
6 In spite of having all the necessary qualifications, they didn't offer Sue the job.
7 Harry did not go to college, nevertheless he made a fortune later in life.
8 As a result the pilots' strike, all flights had to be canceled.
9 Whereas the new system is extremely simple, the old one was very complicated.
10 I walked into the room quietly so as not waking her up.

◀ Go back to page 53

105

GRAMMAR PRACTICE

7A Verb patterns (2): reporting

 7.6
Eric **told me that he wanted** to move abroad.
She **wondered if we were leaving** on our trip soon.
Phil **urged me to talk** to my teacher.
My parents **say a college education** opens doors.
We **demanded that she listen** to us.
My teacher **suggested that we go** to the lecture.

Verb patterns

When we report what someone said, we can report a statement, a question, or a command. We usually use verbs such as *say*, *tell*, *explain*, *admit*, *mention*, and *report*.

In most cases, we change the tense of the verb in reported speech.

"I love to swim." ⇨ *He said (that) he loved to swim.*
"I've been reading a lot." ⇨ *Ann told me (that) she'd been reading a lot.*

When the verb is a modal, we change the tense of *can*, *will*, and *may*. However, we don't change the tense of *would*, *could*, *might*, and *should*.

"I can speak Hindi." ⇨ *Laura mentioned (that) she could speak Hindi.*
"I might go to the movies." ⇨ *George said (that) he might go to the movies.*

We report a *Yes/No* question with an affirmative form of the verb. When we report a *Wh-* question, we include the question word(s) instead of *if/whether*.

"Do you want to read the paper?" ⇨ *She asked (me) if I wanted to read the paper.*
"Where are you going?" ⇨ *He asked (us) where we were going.*

We use an infinitive to report the verbs *allow*, *permit*, *agree*, *persuade*, *urge*, *refuse*, *enable*, *encourage*, *threaten*, *beg*, *promise*, *want*, and *expect*.

"You really need to see a doctor." ⇨ *My friends persuaded me to see a doctor.*
"Don't leave!" ⇨ *They begged me not to leave.*

The present

We sometimes report what someone said very recently. In these cases, the tense does not usually change. The reporting verb can also be in the present.

"I want to talk to Jane after class." ⇨ *He says he wants to talk to you after class.*

We also use the present to report a fact or something that is relevant now.

"It's cold up north in the winter!" ⇨ *John said it's cold up north in the winter!*
"You play the piano pretty well." ⇨ *Linda said I play the piano pretty well.*

Subjunctive uses

Some reporting verbs are followed by the subjunctive form of the verb, particularly in formal speech. We can use a subjunctive form after *advise*, *ask*, *command*, *demand*, *desire*, *insist*, *prefer*, *recommend*, *request*, *suggest*, and *urge*.

The subjunctive form of the verb is an infinitive without *to*. For a negative subjunctive, add "not" before the infinitive.

They advised that she come 15 minutes early.
We suggested that the website be updated.
I requested that the mailman not leave me junk mail.

In informal speech, we avoid using the subjunctive. Instead, we can use an infinitive or *should*.

They advised us to come early.
They recommended that we should come early.

---

1 Check (✓) the correct examples of reporting *in italics* and correct any mistakes.

Hi Brenda,

Remember ¹*I told you I'd been thinking of leaving* my job, breaking up with Tom, and starting a new life in Buenos Aires? Well, I've made up my mind, and I'm leaving next month!

Yesterday I finally told Tom the news. At first, he just laughed and ²*said I am joking*, but when he realized our relationship was really over, he ³*begged me to don't go*. I didn't know what to say, so I ⁴*asked him if could we still be friends*, which made things worse. He ⁵*refused to even listen* to me and ⁶*said he never wanted* to see me again. ☹

Anyway, I'd never expected Tom to take the news well, but I was sure Mom and Dad would be more supportive. I was wrong! They made a list of all the things that could go wrong and ⁷*urged me thinking it over*. Dad even ⁸*reminded me that I had* a good job at ABC, and my parents ⁹*say that good jobs were hard to find*.

Text me! Love Ana

2 Complete the sentences with the correct form of the verbs in parentheses.

1 I suggest that Geoff _____ a few more driving lessons before his test. (take)
2 "I didn't catch that, dear." "Mom _____ you _____ a new hearing aid, Bill." (say, need)
3 Mrs. Robinson demanded that her car _____ immediately as she would need it later that day. (be, repair)
4 The tour guide insisted that the tourists _____ the sculptures at the museum. (not touch)
5 The scientist explained that water _____ at 100°C at sea level. (boil)
6 The doctor recommended that Peter _____ his daily fat intake. (reduce)
7 The sign at the pool recommended that young children _____ by an adult. (be accompany)
8 My teacher mentioned that I _____ really good at analytical thinking. (be)

◀ Go back to page 59

7C Future time

  7.9

By the end of the year, I **will be living** in Los Angeles.
A year from now, **we won't have bought** a house yet.
By the time I see you, I **will have been working** at my new job for six months.
We **won't have been living** here very long when school starts.
The last time we talked, you **were going** to spend the summer in Mexico.
Tim **was leaving** the day after tomorrow, so I'm sure he's still here.

Future continuous

We use the future continuous to predict events and plans that will be in progress at a certain point in the future.

A year from now, I'll be living in New York.
I won't be able to call you at 3 p.m. since I'll be driving.

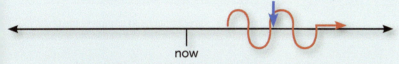

Future perfect

We use the future perfect to predict events that will be completed before a certain point in the future. We can also use *may* or *might* to express a possibility.

By next year, we will have doubled our sales.
The package won't have arrived by the weekend.
We might not have found a place to live by the time you come to visit.

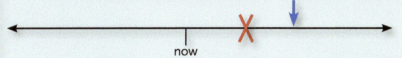

Future perfect continuous

We use the future perfect continuous to predict events that will be in progress at a certain point in the future. The focus is on the period of time the event is in progress before the point in the future.

By January, we will have been trying this strategy for six months.
By December, I will have been working here for six months.

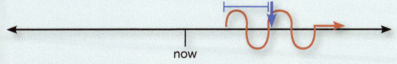

We use the future perfect continuous with *How long ... ? For ...* , and *Since ...* , but we may also use the future perfect. We don't use the simple present/present continuous.

How long will you have been living/have lived here by the time you graduate?
I will have been living/lived here for six years. NOT ~~I'm living/I live~~.

The future in the past

We use the past continuous or *going to* to say what plans, intentions, or predictions we had at a certain point in the past.

David was leaving the next day to see his mother.
Amy was going to start nursing school the last time I saw her.

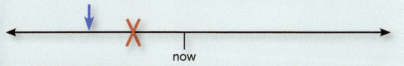

GRAMMAR PRACTICE

1 Complete the conversations with the correct form of the verbs in parentheses.

1. **A** Do you think Johnny will have trouble with Spanish when he goes to Chile?
   B I'm sure he'll get by. I mean, by next month, he _____ Spanish for six months. (study)
2. **A** Is Elsa going to pick us up at the station?
   B She _____ for us when our train arrives. At least, that's what she said. (wait)
3. **A** Sorry, I'm late! I got stuck in traffic. Can we still make it to the party?
   B I don't think so. By the time we get there, everyone _____ . (already / leave)
4. **A** Juan has been to six different countries this year!
   B At this rate, he _____ every country in the world by the time he's 40! (visit)
5. **A** _____ Celine for lunch tomorrow? (you / see)
   B Yes, probably. Why?
6. **A** Do you think you _____ by the time you're 65? (retire)
   B I doubt it. I think I _____ full time. (still / work)
7. **A** Can you believe this airline?
   B I know! We _____ for almost two hours when our plane finally arrives. (wait)
8. **A** When we arrive in New York, we'll need to get some rest.
   B I know. We _____ almost 400 miles! (drive)

2 In each pair, check (✓) the sentence that uses the past continuous to talk about the future in the past.

1. a Barry was very nervous because he was getting married that morning.
   b When I spoke to Luke this morning, he was getting ready to go to work.
2. a I saw Tim, who was leaving the next day.
   b I was leaving home when the phone rang.
3. a Sorry, I completely forgot we were having lunch today.
   b We were having lunch when we heard the news.

3 Complete the sentences with the past continuous or *going to* form of the words in the box. More than one answer may be possible.

be   buy   call   say   study

1. Sorry! I _____ you today, but I forgot.
2. I just knew Mom _____ the wrong thing and embarrass me in front of my friends.
3. I _____ a new car the next day, so I gave away my old one.
4. I had a feeling the meeting _____ a disaster. Turns out I was right.
5. The last time I talked to you, you _____ German. Did you do it?

◀ Go back to page 63

GRAMMAR PRACTICE

8A Relative clauses with quantifiers and prepositions

 8.2

We're going for dinner at Brannigans, **which** is a great restaurant near my house.
I read the instructions, **all of which** were in English.
She introduced me to her friends, **none of whom** I'd met before.
They're the neighbors **who** we had the barbecue **with**.
The person **to whom** I owe the most is my grandmother.

Non-defining relative clauses with quantifiers

A non-defining relative clause gives us extra information about something in the main clause. We can use a quantifier with a non-defining relative clause to specify part of a group. These relative clauses begin with, e.g., *all*, *most*, *both*, *some*, *a few*, *none*.

Our sales representatives, a few of whom you know, are here to help.
He tells a lot of good stories, none of which are true.

A non-defining relative clause with a quantifier can follow either a countable or an uncountable noun.

I'd like to introduce you to my cousins, a few of whom you've met before. (countable)
This medicine, a little of which will really help you, is pretty affordable. (uncountable)

> **Look!** We cannot use a direct object pronoun after the word *of*.
> *Our professors, all of whom are very committed, work very long hours.*
> NOT *Our professors, all of them are very committed, work very long hours.*

We can also use ordinal numbers and superlatives to quantify part of a group.

There are a number of rules here, the first of which is very important.
I have two sisters, the youngest of whom is starting school next week.

The fixed expressions *in which case*, *by which time*, and *at which point* can also be used to form non-defining relative clauses.

I think it's going to rain tomorrow, in which case we should stay in.
We're meeting at 6:00 p.m., by which time I will have finished work.
The movie ended, at which point the audience all started to clap.

Relative clauses with prepositions

If there is a verb in a relative clause that needs a preposition, the preposition is usually at the end of the clause. This can happen in both defining and non-defining relative clauses.

The man who I sold my car to called me yesterday. (defining)
John told me a good joke, which I had to laugh at. (non-defining)

In formal speech, the preposition comes before the relative pronoun. The relative pronoun *who* changes to *whom*.

A few years ago, he had an accident, from which he never really recovered.
This house, for which we paid a good deal of money, has been very problematic.
The professor to whom I owe my scholarship is retiring next year.

1 Rewrite the sentences, combining the two sentences into one.

1 My classmates are all teenagers. Most of them are from Spain.
___
2 I have four jackets. None of them fits me now!
___
3 I have two brothers. The oldest just started his own business.
___
4 There were 30 exam questions. The first was very difficult.
___
5 I spoke to the manager. She was apologetic.
___

2 Choose the correct options to complete the text.

> We've all seen those websites [1] *that / —* feature "the world's most inspirational places," most of [2] *them / which* are hundreds of miles away. But I've found places [3] *in I feel at home / I feel at home in* when I want to be inspired, right near where I live. Here are just three inspirational urban locations, [4] *all / all of which* are completely free to visit.
>
> 1 The library I am a member [5] *— / of* has over 100,000 books, [6] *which / that* makes me feel very lucky to live here!
>
> 2 I live near the train station, [7] *that / which* is a great place to watch people. My friend Camille, who I often hang out [8] *— / with*, likes drawing the people she sees there.
>
> 3 There are three parks in my city, the biggest [9] *of which / —* has a lake and gardens. I like to lie down, close my eyes, and just smell the flowers!

◀ Go back to page 67

108

8C Mixed conditionals and alternatives to *if*

 8.10

If you **hadn't woken** me up, **I'd** still **be** asleep now!
If she **was** a better student, she **would have done** better on her exams.
Make sure you fill out this form. **Otherwise**, you won't be paid.
I'm not going to speak to Karl again, **whether** he apologizes **or not**!
Provided we watch our expenses, we'll be able to save money.

Mixed conditionals

We can use a mixed conditional to describe an unreal condition in the past and a present consequence. We form the *if* clause with *if* + past perfect, and the main clause with *would* + infinitive.

If the car hadn't broken down, we would be home now.
If I'd been on time for my last interview, I'd have the job.

We can describe a future consequence using *would* or *could*.

If Lucy hadn't broken her leg, she could come skiing with us.

We can also use a mixed conditional to describe an unreal condition in the present and a past consequence. We form the *if* clause with *if* + simple past, and the main clause with *would have* + past participle.

If you lived nearer, I would have walked here.
If I spoke French better, we wouldn't have taken the wrong train in Paris.

Alternatives to *if*

We can use *as long as*, *so long as*, and *provided* as alternatives in first conditional sentences.

As long as/So long as you're home on time, I won't worry.
Provided you call me in advance, I'll pick you up.

We may use alternatives to *if* in perfect sentences to emphasize that one action occurs before another. *Provided* and *so long as* are more formal than *as long as*.

Students may leave the exam early provided (so long as/as long as) they have completed each section of the paper.

We can use *suppose* and *supposing* to imagine both possible and unlikely conditions.

Supposing they don't arrive on time, what will you do?
Suppose we offered you more money, would you agree to stay?

In more formal speech and writing, we can form a third conditional by removing *if* and inverting the subject and *had*.

Had there been more time, we could have visited the museum. = If there had been more time, he could have visited the museum.

We can use *otherwise* as an alternative to *if not*.

You'll have to lend me your laptop. Otherwise/If not, I won't be able to finish my assignment.

We use *whether … or not* to refer to two possibilities at once.

I'm going to sell the car, whether you agree or not/whether or not you agree.
(= either way, if you agree or if you don't agree)

GRAMMAR PRACTICE

1 Rewrite the sentences, combining the two sentences into one. Use *if*.

1 I'm scared of insects. I didn't catch the wasp.
If I wasn't scared of insects, I would have caught the wasp.

2 This country is cold. We couldn't camp outside last night.
_____

3 You stayed up late last night. You're tired today.
_____

4 The government didn't prepare for the financial crisis. The economy is in trouble.
_____

5 The kids were naughty. They're not allowed to watch TV tonight.
_____

6 She failed her exams. She's retaking them next week.
_____

7 I live in a dangerous area. I was mugged.
_____

8 I wasn't paying attention yesterday in the parking lot. My car is scratched.
_____

2 Combine the sentences using the words in parentheses. Make any other changes necessary.

1 Call a taxi. If you don't, we'll have to walk. (otherwise)
Call a taxi; otherwise, we'll have to walk.

2 You can go out this afternoon. You have to be back in time for dinner. (as long as)
_____

3 Phones may be brought into the building. They need to be switched to silent mode, though. (provided)
_____

4 I don't know if my team will win. I always enjoy the game, though. (whether or not)
_____

5 Imagine that the world might end tomorrow. What would you do with your final day? (supposing)
_____

6 We weren't aware of the situation. As a result, we couldn't act differently. (had)
_____

7 It's supposed to be sunny tomorrow. If not, I don't think I'll go to the beach. (otherwise)
_____

8 It's not impossible to have an earthquake here. What precautions have you taken? (suppose)
_____

◀ Go back to page 71

109

GRAMMAR PRACTICE

9A Participle clauses

 9.2

Looking over my shoulder, I noticed someone behind me.
The website **selling** tickets has stopped working.
While packing my bag, I realized I didn't have my passport.
The car belongs to a woman **named** Sarah Malone.
Translated into 20 languages, it's one of the most popular books in the world.
Having introduced himself, Bill decided to sit next to me.
Being such a good student, Sarah doesn't usually study much for her exams.

We use participle clauses to make our speech more efficient as they allow us to omit words. They are also used to add extra information.

Present participles to give extra information

A present participle clause is sometimes a shortened or reduced relative clause.

Who is that man who is talking to my sister?
I'd like a ticket for the movie which is starting at 7:30.

Present participles can also work as adverbials. They express meanings such as manner, cause, result, or time.

Listening carefully, I was able to understand what she said.
Being quite shy, she didn't talk much at first.

Present participles are often used after conjunctions and prepositions.

While traveling across the country, she became sick.
After paying the check, we left the restaurant and went for a walk.

> **Look!** A participle clause must have the same subject as the main clause.
> *Driving my daughter to school, I noticed she'd fallen asleep.* NOT *Driving my daughter to school, she fell asleep.*

Past participles to give extra information

Past participles are generally used to express a passive meaning.

Built in 1974, this building is the tallest in the city.
Covered with melted chocolate, this fruit makes a delicious snack.
Praised by her teacher, Lucy felt really happy all day.

A past participle clause may also be a reduced relative clause.

She was wearing the dress which was given to her by her father.
My English teacher, who is admired by all her students, is really fantastic.

Perfect participles to show a sequence of events

We can use a perfect participle to emphasize that one action happened before another.

Having boarded the plane, we both fell asleep.
Having spoken to our teacher, I know I did well on the exam.

If there are more than two actions in the sequence, only use the perfect participle for the first action.

Having boarded the plane, we both fell asleep and didn't wake up until landing.

---

1 Choose the correct options to complete the sentences.

1. Carrying the box downstairs, *I suddenly dropped it / it suddenly fell to the floor*.
2. On the living room wall is a beautiful picture *painting by a local artist / painted by a local artist*.
3. We got lost soon after arriving in Paris, *having never been there before / having never being there before*.
4. Taken care of properly, *you'll keep these plants / these plants will live* for a long time.
5. She's been in a really good mood since *met him / meeting him*.
6. While listening to music, *I cleaned the house / the house was cleaned* yesterday.

2 Replace the phrases in **bold** with a participle clause. Combine the sentences when necessary.

1. **I'm from Nigeria**. I'm used to hot weather.
2. **After they filled the car with gas**, they drove to Florida.
3. The community is very proud of its block parties, **which are held every year in June**.
4. Do you recognize that woman **who is crossing the street**?
5. **He didn't want to upset her**. He agreed to meet at the restaurant.
6. They left the theater **after they slept through the entire movie**.

3 Complete the text using the words in the box.

> embarrassed   feeling   frightened
> having bought   having reached
> having worked   hoping   realizing
> running   thinking

¹_____ until very late, I was walking home in the dark, ²_____ tired and hungry. I went into a little grocery, ³_____ to find something to eat. ⁴_____ some snacks, I left the store and continued walking home. After a while, ⁵_____ a park, I suddenly heard someone yelling. I turned around and there was a guy ⁶_____ toward me and yelling, "Your wallet!" ⁷_____ by him, I started running, too. But the man was faster than me and soon caught up. ⁸_____ I was being mugged, I put my hand in my pocket to find my wallet. And that's when the man handed it to me! ⁹_____ I had left it in the store, I took my wallet and apologized, utterly ¹⁰_____ by my behavior!

◀ Go back to page 77

9C Past forms for unreal situations

 9.7

What if we **asked** Simon to come with us?
If only we **'d known** that yesterday!
I wish you **were** a little more patient.
I wish he **wasn't leaving** so early.
It's about time she **apologized**!
We**'d rather** you **didn't mention** this to anyone.

what if/if only

We use *what if* to imagine a situation or to make a suggestion. To talk about the present and future, we use *what if* + simple past. To talk about the past, we use *what if* + past perfect.

What if we met at 6:30 instead of at 7:00?
What if you'd fallen and broken your leg?

We use *if only* to express a strong desire for change in the present or future, or to express regret about something that didn't happen in the past.

If only we had a car!
If only you'd told me earlier!

wish

Wish has the same meaning as *if only* but is a little less strong. To talk about the present and future, we use *wish* + simple past. To talk about the past, we use *wish* + past perfect.

I wish it wasn't so cold today!
I wish I hadn't left the party early!

We can also use *would* after *wish* and *if only*. We use *would* to complain about things we find annoying.

If only you would clean up sometimes! = *If only you cleaned up sometimes!*
I wish you wouldn't yell so often! = *I wish you didn't yell so often!*

> **Look!** Don't use *would* with *wish* or *if only* to talk about yourself. Instead, use *could*.
> *I wish/If only I could speak Spanish!* NOT *I wish/If only I ~~would~~ speak Spanish!*

would rather

We use *would rather* + simple past to talk about preference, now or in the future. To express regret about something that didn't happen, we use the past perfect.

My teacher would rather we tried to answer questions, even if we get them wrong.
Patricia wants to go to the movies tonight, but I'd rather she stayed at home.
I'd rather you had checked with me beforehand.

It's (about) time

We use *It's time* + simple past to express a wish for something to happen in the present or future, which hasn't happened yet or isn't happening now. We use *It's about time* or *It's high time* for added emphasis.

It's time you learned to drive.
It's about time/It's high time you left!

GRAMMAR PRACTICE

1 Check (✓) the correct sentences and correct any mistakes.
   1 I wish I was rich! I would buy a sports car.
   2 If only I would play the guitar!
   3 I'd rather you don't have to leave.
   4 It's about time he listened to what his boss says.
   5 If only you came last weekend! It was so much fun.
   6 I'm exhausted! If only I had gone to bed earlier last night.
   7 It's about time you had gotten ready! We're already late.
   8 I wish you wouldn't play that loud music late at night!

2 Complete the sentences with the correct form of the verbs in parentheses.
   1 I wish you _____ here yesterday. You'd have loved it! (be)
   2 If only you _____ to see things from my point of view. (try)
   3 My parents would rather I _____ so lazy, but it's just the way I am. (not be)
   4 It's high time the government _____ this mess. (straighten out)
   5 I can't believe you cheated on the exam! What if someone _____ you? (see)
   6 What if you _____ the chance to go to the moon? Would you take it? (have)

3 Rewrite the sentences to express the same ideas using the words in parentheses. Make any changes necessary.
   1 Let's go out for dinner tomorrow. We haven't done that in a while. (what if)
   2 I want my daughter to listen to me, but she doesn't! (wish)
   3 That's a little late. I'd prefer for you to come at 6:30. (would rather)
   4 I didn't study for my exam. What a mistake! (wish)
   5 My teacher said she wanted me to repeat French again this summer. (would rather)
   6 Look at what the puppy's done! We shouldn't have forgotten to close the living room door. (if only)

◀ Go back to page 81

GRAMMAR PRACTICE

10A Distancing language

 10.3

It has been announced that there will be a new library built next year.
The dollar **is expected to** fall against the euro.
My suitcase **is believed to** have been misplaced.
According to the news, there's going to be a storm tomorrow.
Lucy and Roger broke up last week, **apparently**.
It seems that there has been a mistake.
The company **appears to be** having financial problems.

We use distancing language when we report information we are not entirely certain of, or to say it is from another source.

Passive structures

We can use the following passive structures to distance ourselves from the information:

- *It* + passive verb + *that* + clause
  Verbs commonly used with this structure include *think, report, announce, suggest, believe, expect,* and *say*.
  It is said that Chinese is a difficult language to learn.
  It has been reported that the Prime Minister will resign soon.

- subject + passive verb + *to* + infinitive
  Verbs commonly used with this structure include *think, report, believe, understand, expect,* and *say*.
  That species of whale was thought to be extinct until last year.
  The actor is believed to be away filming in Panama.

- *There* + passive verb + *to* + infinitive
  There are said to be many more species at risk of extinction.
  There is expected to be another election before the end of the year.

Distancing expressions

We use the expressions *according to* and *apparently* to report information. We use *according to* to specify a source, but we may not be sure if the information is true. We use *apparently* to report information without specifying a source.

Louise is going to leave her job, according to what Sam says.
According to Spanish television, a new midfielder will join Real Madrid next summer.
Apparently, there are more stars in the galaxy than people in the world.
Bus drivers are going on strike tomorrow, apparently.

appear/seem

We can also use *seem* and *appear* to distance ourselves from the information.
Jan seems to be upset.
It appears that his car has been stolen.

To further distance ourselves from the information, we can use *It would seem that* and *It would appear that*. These are both more formal.
It would seem that Jan is upset.
It would appear that his car has been stolen.

Look! We use a perfect infinitive to talk about the past.
The thieves are believed to have robbed at least three banks.
There appears to have been a problem with your credit card.

1 Rewrite each sentence with distancing language, beginning with the word(s) given. In passive sentences, use a form of the same verbs as in the first sentence.

1 Paul says we have a meeting in five minutes.
According _____ .
2 I heard he didn't go out last night because he was at Christina's house.
Apparently _____ .
3 Gloria suggested she had something better to do.
It appears _____ .
4 They think the weather is a little warmer today.
The weather _____ .
5 The report says that the war ended last year.
The war _____ .
6 The government believes that the economy is stronger than ever.
The economy _____ .
7 People think there are only five different types of personalities.
There are _____ .
8 Statistics have suggested that crime is lower this year.
It has _____ .

2 Complete the text with the words in the box.

| according | apparently | appear | estimated |
| have | is | reported | there | to |

It has been ¹_____ that a farmer in the north of the country has made a very important discovery. There ²_____ to be coins and items of jewelry from over a thousand years ago. The discovery ³_____ understood to have taken place while the farmer was digging a well. According ⁴_____ historians, it is one of the most significant finds of recent years, and the jewelry is ⁵_____ by experts to be worth more than a million dollars. The discovery seems to ⁶_____ caused a great deal of excitement, and ⁷_____ is believed to be a lot of interest from both the national museum and private collectors. ⁸_____ to his family, the farmer is extremely happy with his discovery, but ⁹_____ has chosen to remain anonymous.

112

◀ Go back to page 85

10C Adverbs and adverbial phrases

 10.11

It's **highly** likely that it will rain.
We finished work **late**.
We visit my grandmother **every other weekend**.
To everyone's amazement, Jenny refused to stand up and speak!
I haven't been well **lately**.
That band is **incredibly** successful.

Common adverb collocations

Adverbs frequently collocate with certain adjectives or verbs. *Deeply* often collocates with emotions, *strongly* with opinions or beliefs, and *highly* with probability.

He was deeply ashamed when he was caught cheating.
I strongly believe that everyone should be given a second chance.
It's highly unlikely that we'll win the game.

Adverbs with two forms

Some adverbs have two forms: one with *-ly* and the other with the adjective form. Sometimes the two forms have similar meanings (*first*, *firstly*; *tight*, *tightly*), but most have different meanings:

hard = a lot of effort	hardly = almost not at all
fair = according to the rules	fairly = moderately
fine = quite well	finely = in small pieces
free = with no charge	freely = with no restriction
high = far above the ground	highly = very, to a great extent
late = after the expected time	lately = recently
most = out of all things	mostly = generally
near = close	nearly = almost
wide = fully, from side to side	widely = a lot
wrong = incorrectly	wrongly = unfairly, unjustly

Adverb position

Different types of adverbs go in different positions: at the beginning of a clause; in the middle (before the main verb but after *to be*); or at the end of the clause.

type of adverb	common positions	examples
comment	beginning or middle	**To my surprise**, they are still together. We **obviously** cannot continue in this way.
time	end	Let's meet **on Tuesday at eight thirty**. We'll deliver it **as soon as possible**.
frequency	middle or end	He **almost always** brings a present. I get angry **every time I see him**.
place	end	They're waiting **in the car behind us**. I saw her **in the corner of the room**.
manner	middle or end	Jan **cleverly** chose the biggest room. She argued her case **persuasively**.
degree	middle	She was **incredibly** amusing. I'd **really** like to say something to her.

GRAMMAR PRACTICE

1 Choose the correct words to complete the sentences.
   1 a She *hard* / *hardly* ever goes out any more.
     b I try *hard* / *hardly*, but I always fail.
   2 a I haven't seen John *late* / *lately*.
     b They arrived *late* / *lately* and missed the show.
   3 a Everything is going *wrong* / *wrongly* today.
     b I was *wrong* / *wrongly* accused of lying.
   4 a Do you live *near* / *nearly* here?
     b Are you *near* / *nearly* finished?
   5 a Chop the garlic *fine* / *finely* before you fry it.
     b We get along *fine* / *finely*, despite having a few arguments.
   6 a Citizens of both countries are allowed to move *free* / *freely* across the border.
     b Students can get into the museum *free* / *freely*.
   7 a The thing she loved *most* / *mostly* about him was his sense of humor.
     b The course is *most* / *mostly* about finance, but we also study history.
   8 a I opened the door *wide* / *widely*, but I still couldn't see anyone.
     b Opinions vary *wide* / *widely* on how the economy is doing.
   9 a The kite was flying *high* / *highly* above the rooftops.
     b I can *high* / *highly* recommend my driving instructor.
   10 a We get along *fair* / *fairly* well, but we're not that close.
      b The team didn't deserve to win since they didn't play *fair* / *fairly*.

2 Rewrite each sentence with the adverbs in parentheses in the correct position. There may be more than one answer.
   1 I check personal e-mails. (very rarely / at work)
   2 The classroom is a mess because students forget to clean their desks. (unfortunately / nearly always)
   3 The issue has been dealt with efficiently. (fairly / until now)
   4 I had forgotten to turn off the heat. (stupidly / in the living room)
   5 The thief distracted her victim. (obviously / intentionally)
   6 She has dealt with the criticism. (to my surprise / reasonably well)
   7 The lead guitarist of the band we saw is talented. (clearly / awfully)
   8 Was that you I saw? (in the last row of the movie theater / the night before last)
   9 I drove. (really / quickly / here)
   10 The train has arrived. (fortunately / at last)

◀ Go back to page 89

113

VOCABULARY PRACTICE

6A Neighbors and community

1 ▶ 6.1 Complete the conversation with words and phrases from the box. Listen and check.

community association   close-knit   homeowner
on a first-name basis   sense of (x2)   tenants

I love my new neighborhood. I live in an incredibly ¹_____ community, where people actually look out for each other.

Yeah? Like how?

There's a ²_____ community here. For example, on our block, there's a ³_____ where residents help each other and keep the neighborhood safe.

And you can get to know people, too, right?

Exactly. This is actually the first time I've ever had neighbors who know me ⁴_____ ! We do all kinds of things together, and this creates a true ⁵_____ belonging.

Sounds as if you're really happy there.

I am. Before I lived in an apartment building and didn't even know the other ⁶_____ . So that's why I decided to become a ⁷_____ .

2 ▶ 6.2 Complete the **bold** expressions in the quotations 1–7 with the correct form of the verbs in the box. Listen and check.

break   come   keep   lend   look   reach   strengthen

"If a natural disaster strikes your community, ¹_____ **out to** your friends, neighbors, and complete strangers. ²_____ **a helping hand**."
Marsha Blackburn, politician

"This is the moment when we must ³_____ **together** to save this planet."
Barack Obama, former U.S. president

"We have to ⁴_____ **an eye on** the future with a sense of the past in every passing moment of the present."
Amanda Harlech, writer

"I've had faith my whole life that there was someone ⁵_____ **out for** me, a spirit guide, a soul guide."
Lady Gaga, singer

"The easiest time to be funny is during a fairly serious situation. That way, you can ⁶_____ **the ice**."
Adam McKay, movie director

"Establishing family rituals and traditions is one effective way to ⁷_____ **family ties**."
Irene Swerdlow-Freed, psychologist

◀ Go back to page 48

6B Word pairs

1 ▶ 6.6 Match 1–10 with a–j. Listen and check.

1 If you do something **time after time**,
2 If you see a situation as **black and white**,
3 If you talk to somebody **one to one**,
4 If something will **make or break** a relationship,
5 If you're prepared to **give and take**,
6 If you're **safe and sound**,
7 If an experience is **short and sweet**,
8 If you say you can **take it or leave it**,
9 If you do something **bit by bit**,
10 If something has **highs and lows**,

a you do it gradually or a little at a time.
b you're willing to compromise and do things for another person.
c you do it many times or repeatedly.
d you speak only to that person.
e it has both good parts and bad parts.
f you see it as clear and simple, although others may see it as complicated.
g you like that thing, but you don't love it or really need it.
h it will either lead to its success or failure.
i it doesn't last long, but is enjoyable.
j you are well and unhurt after being in a dangerous situation.

2 Complete sentences 1–10 with the phrases in **bold** in exercise 1.
1 I couldn't cook at all when I left home, but _____ I learned the basic techniques.
2 There were a few scary moments on our hike, but we all got back _____ .
3 I enjoy talking to my friends _____ more than talking to them in groups.
4 The course has had its _____ , but, overall, I've enjoyed it.
5 She has a _____ view of the situation and doesn't see that many factors are involved.
6 The speech was _____ . It was over in minutes!
7 You need a lot of _____ in any relationship, but especially in marriage.
8 I have told him my name _____ , but he always forgets it.
9 The new online retail system will _____ our company. We've invested so much money in it.
10 My husband is crazy about soccer, but I can _____ .

◀ Go back to page 50

123

VOCABULARY PRACTICE

7A Technology

1 ▶ 7.1 Match the words in the box with pictures a–h. Listen and check.

> attachment   charge a battery   cursor   plug in   scroll up / down   swipe right / left   unplug   wireless network

a _____

b _____

c _____

d _____

e _____

f _____

g _____

h _____

2 ▶ 7.2 Complete the sentences with the correct form of the words in the box. Listen and check.

> broadband   browser   bug   database   device   install   log in / out   undo

1 Today, fast and reliable _____ connectivity for your home is as important as electricity itself.
2 I've never understood why all electronic _____ have to be turned off during takeoff and landing.
3 If you press Control + Z in Windows (Command + Z on a Mac), you can _____ your last action, which is useful if you make a mistake.
4 My company has _____ new software to keep its client _____ up-to-date.
5 I don't understand why I'm having trouble _____ . My password is correct, so it's probably some kind of _____ .
6 I have several _____ to connect to the Internet, but I prefer Firefox.

3 ▶ 7.3 Match the words in **bold** with definitions a–f. Listen and check.

1 I wouldn't want to **work remotely**. I think I'd miss interacting face to face with my manager and coworkers.
2 The hospital uses **state-of-the-art** technology to treat patients with high-quality care.
3 I'm the only **computer-literate** person in the family, so everyone is always asking me for help.
4 Videos and high definition images consume more **bandwidth** than text does.
5 I get mad at myself when I lose work because I've forgotten to **back** it **up**.
6 If you open too many programs at the same time, the computer might run out of memory and **crash**.

a familiar with the operation of computers
b the transmission capacity for data transfer on a computer network
c make a copy of computer data to protect against accidental damage or loss
d the most modern available
e carry out job responsibilities from a distance
f suddenly stop working or fail

◀ Go back to page 58

VOCABULARY PRACTICE

7C Expressions with *world* and *place*

1 ▶ 7.8 Complete the conversations with the expressions in the boxes. Listen and check.

> all over the place   takes place   it's a small world

A So, did you enjoy the book?
B Yes, the plot was great. There were some old words I had to look up, though.
A I'm not surprised. The story ¹_____ in the 18th century, remember? Did you see the movie?
B No. Was it any good?
A Not really. I hated the acting, and visually it was ²_____. It's as if the director tried to mix two different centuries. But I did run into Jo from high school at the theater!
B ³_____!

> fall into place   in first place   thinks the world of
> it's not the end of the world

A I was let go this morning.
B Oh, no! I'm sorry to hear that. Losing your job is hard, I know, but ⁴_____. I mean, I'm sure you'll find something.
A I guess so. Things will ⁵_____ eventually, I hope.
B I'm sure they will. Don't forget to ask Julie for a letter of recommendation. She ⁶_____ you, so I'm sure she'll be happy to write one.
A I saw Julie the other day at the tennis tournament. She was ⁷_____ when I saw her. I'm not sure if she won in the end, though.

> in the first place   out of this world   worlds apart

A Hey, welcome back! Did you have a good time?
B Thanks. Yeah, but the hotel was such a disappointment – ⁸_____ from the place where we stayed last year. Now, that was a good hotel. And the food was ⁹_____, too.
A So why did you choose a different hotel ¹⁰_____?

◀ Go back to page 62

8A Science and discovery: word families

1 ▶ 8.1 Complete the chart with the correct form of each word. Listen and check.

noun	adjective	verb
evidence		evidence (formal)
	hypothetical	hypothesize
experiment	experimental	
analysis		analyze
	proven	prove
conclusion	conclusive	
influence		influence
	theoretical	theorize
evaluation	evaluative	
inspiration		inspire
	innovative	innovate
classification	classified	

2 Complete the sentences. Use the correct form of the words in the chart in exercise 1. The first letter is given for you.

1 Scientists usually break down problems into smaller parts. They are **a**_____ thinkers.
2 The reference books are in a row and are **c**_____ by subject: chemistry, physics, or biology.
3 In order to convince the scientific community, Dr. Gargav must **p**_____ that his results were not accidental.
4 My chemistry teacher is the reason I became fascinated by science. She was such an **i**_____ to me.
5 The universe is even bigger than we previously thought, according to new **e**_____ from a scientific study.
6 We will have to perform more tests in order to be certain because the results of the laboratory tests were not **c**_____.
7 Rather than using traditional methods, biologists are finding **i**_____ ways to discover how these animals survive.
8 For every new technological discovery, we must **e**_____ the costs against the potential usefulness of the item.

◀ Go back to page 66

VOCABULARY PRACTICE

8B Nouns from phrasal verbs

1 ▶ 8.5 Replace the underlined parts of sentences 1–10 with the words in the box. Listen and check.

> backup   breakdown   breakup   catch-up   giveaway
> let-down   mix-up   outbreak   takeoff   workout

1 I have very little free time, so I'm always playing a game trying to keep up with the housework.   _____
2 There was a mistake with our tickets, so we got the wrong ones.   _____
3 The link to a free download of her album was a great free gift after the concert.   _____
4 I sometimes feel pretty lonely after a relationship ends.   _____
5 His first novel was fantastic, but his second was a disappointment.   _____
6 We're having an outdoor wedding, but if it rains, we've rented a huge tent as a replacement if our main plans go wrong.   _____
7 This detailed list of tasks says that the next thing to do is get a report from our attorney.   _____
8 After the sudden start of war, thousands of people left their homes in search of safety.   _____
9 We boarded the plane on time, but then the plane's departure was delayed for an hour.   _____
10 I like having a period of physical exercise after a whole day sitting at a desk.   _____

◀ Go back to page 68

9A Friendship and love

1 ▶ 9.1 Match phrases 1–14 with definitions a–n. Listen and check.

1 bond (over something)
2 date someone
3 drift apart
4 get along like a house on fire
5 go back a long way
6 hang out (with someone)
7 have a crush (on someone)
8 have someone's back
9 love at first sight
10 platonic relationship
11 see eye to eye
12 settle down
13 soulmate
14 hit it off

a immediately get along well with someone new
b agree or have the same opinion on a topic
c gradually become less connected with a friend
d have a strong romantic interest in someone
e fall in love when you first see or meet someone
f establish a link with someone as a result of shared interests
g have known someone for a long time
h go out with someone you are romantically interested in
i a friendship with no romantic involvement
j be ready and willing to support someone if necessary
k spend time with someone, relaxing and enjoying yourself
l a person perfectly suited as a close friend or romantic partner
m get along really well with someone
n to start living in a place where you intend to stay for a long time, usually to start a family

2 Complete the text with the correct form of the phrases in exercise 1. The first letter is given for you.

Janice and I have known each other for over 10 years, so we ¹g_____ . We met in college and immediately ²h_____ , partly because we ³b_____ over our love for the same TV shows! We ⁴h_____ a lot, just watching TV or cooking dinner, but there was never any romance, at first – it was a completely ⁵p_____ . After college I moved to a different city, and we ⁶d_____ , but two years ago, Janice sent me a message, and we made plans to get together. Something was different when we saw each other again. I realized I ⁷h_____ on her! And even better, she felt the same way! So we started ⁸d_____ , and it went incredibly well. We still ⁹g_____ , joking and laughing all the time, but, of course, our relationship is so much more than that now. She's my ¹⁰s_____ ! We don't ¹¹s_____ on everything, in fact, we argue pretty often, but I know that she always ¹²h_____ , and that support is really important. Things are going so well that we're thinking about ¹³s_____ and having children. And when our children ask me, "Daddy, was it ¹⁴l_____ with you and Mommy?" I'll say, "No, we were just friends for years!"

◀ Go back to page 76

126

VOCABULARY PRACTICE

9C Commonly confused words

1 ▶ 9.6 Choose the correct words to complete the sentences. Listen and check.

1 a Some people like working in groups, but I prefer to work *lonely / alone*.
  b You live by yourself, don't you? Don't you ever feel *lonely / alone*?
2 a I feel uncomfortable when someone pays me a *compliment / complement*. I just don't know what to say!
  b You should paint this wall green. It would really *compliment / complement* the blue carpet.
3 a There was a car parked *beside / besides* the road. I think it must have broken down.
  b I didn't call you because I didn't have your number. *Beside / Besides* you wouldn't have come anyway!
4 a The president could have ignored the criticism or reacted to it. He seems to have chosen the *later / latter* option.
  b We've missed the start of the movie, so let's try to see a *later / latter* show.
5 a There's been a slight *rise / raise* in the level of violent crime this year.
  b The guard heard a noise and decided to *rise / raise* the alarm.
6 a You need to calm down. You're not being *rational / rationale*!
  b I know what you think the company should do, but I don't understand your *rational / rationale*.
7 a I'm starting college next week, and I need some notebooks, pencils, and other *stationery / stationary*.
  b The woman whose car I crashed into said her car was *stationery / stationary* at the moment of impact, but, in fact, she was moving at about 10 km./h.
8 a There is a meeting tomorrow at 9 a.m., and everyone will *assist / attend*.
  b Please let me know if I can *assist / attend* you in any way.
9 a I really *benefitted / profited* from my investment, as the stock market continued to rise.
  b To be honest, I think you would both *benefit / profit* from some time apart from each other.
10 a The two sides need to reach a *compromise / commitment* eventually, but they are currently a long way from finding any area of agreement.
  b We made a *compromise / commitment* to support our business during difficult times, and we are going to honor that.

2 Complete the e-mail with the words in the box.

> attend   benefit   besides   complement   compromise   later   raise   rational

To: Mariella Mendham
From: Birgit Tandon
Subject: Sinton project

Dear Mariella,

Have you had a chance to consider who you would like to work with on the Sinton project? I plan to ¹_____ the issue ²_____ with senior management, and it would be good to know your thoughts. Have you considered Martin? I think your people skills would really ³_____ his knowledge of the field, and you would certainly ⁴_____ from his experience. ⁵_____ , I know you work well together, and so it would be a very ⁶_____ decision. However, you may have someone else in mind. If we don't agree on who would be the best partner for you, I'm sure we can find some sort of ⁷_____ . Anyhow, let me know what you think, and please confirm whether or not you plan to ⁸_____ the meeting this afternoon?

Thanks very much, and I look forward to hearing from you.

Birgit

◀ Go back to page 80

VOCABULARY PRACTICE

10A Humans and self

1 ▶ 10.1 Match words and phrases 1–8 with definitions a–h. Listen and check.

1	humane	a	cruel and without sympathy
2	human nature	b	the things every person is entitled to by law
3	human rights	c	the department of a business involved in hiring and training of staff
4	human beings	d	having or showing compassion and sympathy
5	inhumane	e	the feelings and behavior shared by all people
6	humankind	f	concerned with or seeking to promote the welfare of people
7	humanitarian	g	men, women, and children of the species Homo sapiens
8	human resources	h	all people considered as a group

2 Complete the text with the correct form of the words and phrases from exercise 1.

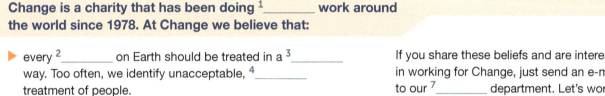

Change is a charity that has been doing ¹_____ work around the world since 1978. At Change we believe that:

▶ every ²_____ on Earth should be treated in a ³_____ way. Too often, we identify unacceptable, ⁴_____ treatment of people.
▶ every single person's ⁵_____ must be protected.
▶ it is not ⁶_____ to be unkind. People are naturally caring and sympathetic.

If you share these beliefs and are interested in working for Change, just send an e-mail to our ⁷_____ department. Let's work together for the good of ⁸_____ .

3 ▶ 10.2 Complete the *self* diagram with the words in the box. Listen and check.

employed   discipline   pity   conscious

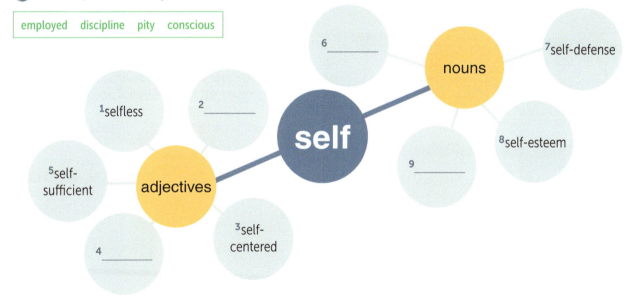

4 Use the *self-* words and expressions to complete the sentences.
1 Sam works so hard for her family and never rests. She's completely _____ .
2 My brother always worries about what people think of what he does or the way he looks. He's very _____ .
3 I worry about my safety outside, so I'm taking a course in _____ .
4 Tim's full of _____ . He's always talking about his awful life and how unlucky he is.
5 Alan has no confidence in his own abilities. He has very low _____ .
6 Unfortunately, my uncle doesn't care about other people. He's completely _____ .
7 I haven't bought anything in ages because I'm saving money. I have pretty good _____ .
8 I'm not surprised Ana's become _____ . She always hated having a boss!
9 Annie is only five, but she gets dressed by herself. She's very _____ .

◀ Go back to page 84

128

VOCABULARY PRACTICE

10B Verbs with re-, over-, mis-

1 ▶ 10.5 Match the verbs in **bold** with definitions a–f. Listen and check.
   1 If you **mistreat** someone, he/she will probably feel hurt and angry.
   2 I **overheard** their conversation. They were speaking very loudly.
   3 This cream is supposed to **rejuvenate** your skin, but it didn't work!
   4 Check your bills carefully as sometimes companies **overcharge** you.
   5 We're working to **restore** the theater after the fire that damaged it.
   6 I used to **misbehave**, and my teachers would tell me off.

   a make something look or feel young again
   b ask somebody for too much money for a product or service
   c act toward someone in a way that isn't acceptable or appropriate
   d return to a former condition or state
   e behave badly
   f hear a conversation between people who aren't talking to you

2 ▶ 10.6 Complete the sentences with the correct form of the verbs in the box. Listen and check.

   | misunderstand   misinterpret   overcome   overestimate   recharge   recreate |

   1 He had a lot of challenges as a teenager, but he _____ them and made a good life for himself.
   2 After my exams, I _____ by taking a couple of weeks' vacation.
   3 I _____ what Leanne said, so I thought her party was this Saturday, not the following one.
   4 We _____ the time it would take to drive there, so we arrived an hour early.
   5 Even when two people speak the same language, they can still _____ what the other says.
   6 The artist has _____ many famous works of art in a modern style.

   ◀ Go back to page 86

10C Adverb collocations

1 ▶ 10.10 Complete the chart with the words in the box. Listen and check.

   | highly   strongly   bitterly   widely |

adverb	+	adjective / verb
1_____		disappointed, regret, resent
deeply		ashamed, embarrassed, concerned, touched
downright		rude, unpleasant
2_____		(un)likely, probable, successful, impressed
incredibly, unbelievably		expensive, cheap, long, short, early, late
mildly		offensive, amusing, irritated, surprised
potentially		fatal, damaging, harmful
seriously, severely		wounded, damaged, injured, criticized
3_____		believe, oppose, support
utterly		astonishing, (un)believable, pointless
vaguely		familiar, aware, remember
4_____		believed, known, used

2 Complete the sentences with an adverb from the chart.
   1 I thought the movie was just _____ amusing, but everyone else thought it was hilarious.
   2 It's _____ pointless trying to get a driver's license. I know I'll fail the test again.
   3 The restaurant was dirty, and the food was disgusting. It's _____ unlikely that we'll go back.
   4 A mosquito bite can be dangerous and even _____ fatal.
   5 I _____ believe that most government programs are designed to help us.
   6 I hope Dan will be OK. He was _____ injured in a motorcycle accident.
   7 We all _____ resent having to work every weekend.
   8 I'm _____ familiar with what's going on in the world, but I don't read the newspaper very often.

◀ Go back to page 89

6A Students A and B

1 Take turns asking each other questions 1–6. Then ask for and give additional information.

> 1 Have you ever missed an important event (test, interview, etc.) because you got held up in traffic?
> 2 Do you know anyone who has recently been fired or laid off?
> 3 When was the last time you had your eyes tested?
> 4 If you could have your bedroom renovated by an interior designer, what would you change?
> 5 Some people hate being given a surprise birthday party. How about you?
> 6 If you were a manager, would you ever hire someone who's extremely smart, but refuses to be told what to do?

COMMUNICATION PRACTICE

6C Student A

1 Read the text. Then cover it and explain your dilemma to Student B. Use linkers to connect your sentences. Student B will respond.

> I teach history in a high school. One of my students, Elise, has always been a great example to the rest of the class. She's really smart, and even though English isn't her first language, she's always been at the top of the class. She's also extremely hardworking and has even come to class sick on occasion so as not to miss anything important. However, on her last essay, she copied entire paragraphs from the Internet! I think she's having family problems, and she might not have had time to come up with her own ideas because of the stress. What should I do? Give her another chance or report her to the principal?

2 Listen to Student B's dilemma and respond. What would you do?

7A Student A

1 Imagine you've been upset about situations 1–3. Describe the situations to Student B and report what you said. Use the prompts below each situation. Then answer Student B's questions.

> 1 Your sister has been out of work for three months, but she still hasn't realized that she needs to change her lifestyle. How did you try to convince her?
> I mentioned …   I recommended …
> 2 You bought a small dog and was told it would stay that way. Six months later, your dog is the size of a Labrador. You called the pet store. What did you say?
> I wondered …   I insisted …
> 3 You accidentally clicked on "reply all," sharing a colleague's secret with over a hundred people. How did you apologize?
> I asked …   I begged …

2 Listen to Student B describe three upsetting situations. Ask questions using the prompts.

> 1 Did you tell …   Did you suggest …
> 2 Did you say …   Did you urge …
> 3 Did you remind …   Did you insist …

7C Students A and B

1 Complete the sentences with information about yourself. Ask follow-up questions and give further information.

1 Next year, I'll have been living in … since … . Personally …
   (Say how you like the neighborhood.)
2 By the end of the day, I'll have spent … online, which …
   (Is this something you're used to doing?)
3 During the last week of December, I'll be … -ing. To be honest, …
   (Are you looking forward to it?)
4 By the end of the year, I'll have been learning how to … for … . I think I …
   (How much progress have you made?)
5 Last year, I was sure I was going to … , but … .
   (What happened?)

COMMUNICATION PRACTICE

7D Student A

1 You and your partner have started an academic tutoring business for high school students. You are both confident that you offer a good service, but business is not going very well. You think the problem is related to marketing. Follow the instructions below to have a conversation with your partner.

Student A	Student B
Suggest the option of advertising in a local newspaper. Explain an advantage of this idea.	Politely disagree with your partner's idea. Explain a disadvantage.
Acknowledge the disadvantage. Invite your partner to suggest an alternative idea.	Suggest the option of advertising on bulletin boards in stores. Explain an advantage of this idea.
Politely disagree with your partner's idea. Explain a disadvantage.	Acknowledge the disadvantage. Invite your partner to suggest an alternative idea.
Suggest the option of handing out leaflets to parents outside schools. Explain an advantage of this idea.	Agree with your partner's idea. Suggest the option of building a social media presence, as well.
Agree with your partner's idea, explaining an advantage of it.	Clarify the two options you have chosen, agreeing that they're the perfect combination.

8A Student A

1 Read facts 1–5 to Student B, completing each sentence with the correct option. Student B will tell you if your answers are correct.

2 Listen to Student B read facts 6–10. The correct answers are in bold. Tell Student B if his/her answers are correct.

1 There are roughly 8.7 million species on Earth, about *500,000 of which / 1 million of which* have been identified so far.

2 Your skin weighs twice as much as your brain, *75% of which / 50% of which* is water.

3 In human history, there have been over 100 billion people, *a quarter of whom / half of whom* have died of malaria.

4 The moon has been visited by 24 people, *8 of whom / 12 of whom* walked on the moon's surface.

5 The average human body contains about 5 liters of blood, *none of which / 0.02% of which* is gold.

6 70% of the world's surface is covered by oceans, **only 5% of which** / 25% of which has been explored by humans.

7 Since life first existed on Earth, there have been billions of species, 49.9% of which / **99.9% of which** are now extinct.

8 Since 1964, the Nobel prize for physics has been awarded to over 100 scientists, **only one of whom has** / only a few of whom have been women.

9 Approximately 3 billion times a year, Earth is struck by lightning bolts, **6,000 of which** / 1,000 of which kill people.

10 Every year, Earth is hit by about a million earthquakes, five of which / **one of which** on average is magnitude 8 or higher.

137

COMMUNICATION PRACTICE

8C Student A

1 Imagine items 1–3 had never been invented. What would have been different in the past? What would be different in the present or future? Discuss your ideas with Student B.

1 cameras

2 the Internet

3 space shuttles

2 Imagine Student B's items had never been invented. Discuss what would be/would have been different.

9A Students A and B

1 Complete the sentences so they are true for you. Change the words in **bold** as necessary.

1 Eaten with a little **mustard**, …
2 Being the **oldest** child in my family, …
3 Coming from a very **cold** climate, …
4 Being a **light** sleeper, …
5 Having gone out **three** nights this week already, …
6 Having studied **English** for several years, …
7 Admired by **almost everyone**, …

9C Student A

1 Read about Shinji's situation.

Shinji is from South Korea and has recently started college in the U.S. Before he left home, he was excited about the experience, but everything has gone wrong. He hasn't met anyone, and he now realizes his English is not as good as he had thought. He struggles to understand what people say, and he's confused about how life works in the U.S. In addition to missing his family and friends back home, he misses the food and culture, and he feels unable to enjoy his new life. His unhappiness has started to affect his studies, too, and he failed his last exam. Now he's very worried. He wants to turn back time and choose a college closer to home.

2 Imagine you are Shinji. Explain your problem to Student B, using the prompts in the box. Listen to Student B's advice and decide on the best thing to do.

| I'd rather …   If only …   It's about time …   I wish … |

3 Listen to Student B describe Olivia's situation. Offer advice.

COMMUNICATION PRACTICE

9D Students A and B

1   Choose four questions to discuss in pairs. State your opinions and support them with reasons, examples, facts, or anecdotes.

  1   Do students who work hard always get good grades in high school and college?
  2   Are you the most organized person in your family?
  3   Where's the best place for a tourist to visit in your country?
  4   Is your generation happier than your parents' generation?
  5   Can most people afford to buy a house in this country?
  6   What's the best place for a great day out in your city?

10A Student A

1   Read about two human behaviors. Think about how you can use the prompts below each text to tell Student B about each behavior.

Why do we blush?

Experts tell us we blush because we know we have done something wrong, and, therefore, we are self-conscious. Blushing is kind of like a physical apology, and everyone understands that we know we did something wrong. Blushing also helps to keep us honest because everyone knows when we're lying. This benefits society.

According to …   Blushing appears …
Blushing is thought to …

Why do we laugh?

We know it is part of human nature to laugh, but did you know there are mainly two types of laughter? The first type is involuntary and happens when we find something very funny. But the second type is much more common. Over 90% of the time, our laughter has nothing to do with something being funny. In these cases, laughter may be used to make social interaction go more smoothly.

There are thought …   Apparently …
This type of laughter seems …

2   Tell Student B about the two behaviors you read about in exercise 1, using the prompts.

3   Listen to Student B answer questions 1–2. Which answer do you find most interesting or surprising?

1 Why do we dream?

2 Why do we make art?

COMMUNICATION PRACTICE

10C Student A

1 Look at the picture and read the story behind it. Note the use of adverbs.

PEOPLE POWER

Something utterly astonishing happened one morning. A man known only as "Andy" was boarding a train in Perth, Australia during rush hour on a Wednesday morning. Because the train was busy, he was standing by the door when suddenly he slipped, and his left leg became stuck between the train and the platform. When the station crew realized what had happened, the first thing they did was instruct the driver not to move. Then they told the man to hold on tight, and they calmly asked other passengers to help them free him. Dozens of passengers worked together, pushing the train back and forth and rocking it until luckily Andy was able to get out. Amazingly, he was not seriously injured. A transportation spokesperson said the man had been saved by "people power" at the right moment.

2 Cover the text and tell Student B the story behind your picture. Use adverbs.

3 Look at Student B's picture and listen to the story behind it. Which story most restores your faith in humanity?

COMMUNICATION PRACTICE

6C Student B

1 Listen to Student A's dilemma and respond. What would you do?

2 Read the text. Then cover it and explain your dilemma to Student A. Use linkers to connect your sentences. Student A will respond.

> I've been studying Spanish with the same group of students for three years, and we've always liked our teachers. Despite their individual differences in teaching style, we've been able to practice speaking a lot in class. Nevertheless, this semester we have a new teacher, Mr. González, and he does all the talking! Unlike my classmates, who have been thinking about complaining to the school's coordinator, I think it would be fairer to speak to Mr. González directly. I'm afraid things might get even worse as a result of the complaint, but then again, we have to do something. What do you think we should do?

7A Student B

1 Listen to Student A describe three upsetting situations. Ask questions with the prompts.

1 Did you tell ...	Did you suggest ...
2 Did you refuse ...	Did you demand ...
3 Did you admit ...	Did you propose ...

2 Imagine you've been upset about situations 1–3. Describe the situations to Student A, and report what you said. Use the prompts below each situation. Then answer Student A's questions.

1 Your sister has been considering dropping out of college to become a singer. You heard her sing, and you thought her voice was awful. How did you try to change her opinion?
I encouraged ...   I explained ...

2 A close friend has been working much too hard lately. You think he's neglecting his family, and you worry about his marriage. What did you say to him?
I told ...   I advised ...

3 You took a final exam last week and the passing grade was 60. You got 59.5. You don't think you deserve to fail the course. How did you try to persuade your teacher?
I mentioned ...   I urged ...

146

COMMUNICATION PRACTICE

7D Student B

1 You and your partner have started an academic tutoring business for high school students. You are both confident that you offer a good service, but business is not going very well. You think the problem is related to marketing. Follow the instructions below to have a conversation with your partner.

Student A
- Suggest the option of advertising in a local newspaper. Explain an advantage of this idea.
- Acknowledge the disadvantage. Invite your partner to suggest an alternative idea.
- Politely disagree with your partner's idea. Explain a disadvantage.
- Suggest the option of handing out leaflets to parents outside schools. Explain an advantage of this idea.
- Agree with your partner's idea, explaining an advantage of it.

Student B
- Politely disagree with your partner's idea. Explain a disadvantage.
- Suggest the option of advertising on bulletin boards in stores. Explain an advantage of this idea.
- Acknowledge the disadvantage. Invite your partner to suggest an alternative idea.
- Agree with your partner's idea. Suggest the option of building a social media presence as well.
- Clarify the two options you have chosen, agreeing that they're the perfect combination.

8A Student B

1 Listen to Student A read facts 1–5. The correct answers are in bold. Tell Student A if his/her answers are correct.

1 There are roughly 8.7 million species on Earth, about *500,000 of which* / **1 million of which** have been identified so far.

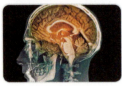

2 Your skin weighs twice as much as your brain, **75% of which** / *50% of which* is water.

3 In human history, there have been over 100 billion people, *a quarter of whom* / **half of whom** have died of malaria.

4 The moon has been visited by 24 people, *8 of whom* / **12 of whom** walked on the moon's surface.

5 The average human body contains about 5 liters of blood, *none of which* / **0.02% of which** is gold.

2 Read facts 6–10 to Student A, completing each sentence with the correct option. Student A will tell you if your answers are correct.

6 70% of the world's surface is covered by oceans, *only 5% of which* / *25% of which* has been explored by humans.

7 Since life first existed on Earth, there have been billions of species, *49.9% of which* / *99.9% of which* are now extinct.

8 Since 1964, the Nobel prize for physics has been awarded to over 100 scientists, *only one of whom has* / *only a few of whom have* been women.

9 Approximately 3 billion times a year, Earth is struck by lightning bolts, *6,000 of which* / *1,000 of which* kill people.

10 Every year, Earth is hit by about a million earthquakes, *five of which* / *one of which* on average is magnitude 8 or higher.

COMMUNICATION PRACTICE

8C Student B

1 Student A will list three items. Imagine the items had never been invented. What would have been different in the past? What would be different in the present or future? Discuss your ideas with Student A.

2 Imagine items 4–6 had never been invented. Discuss what would be/would have been different.

4 airplanes

5 cell phones

6 electric lights

9C Student B

1 Read about Olivia's situation.

Olivia has worked for the same company since she graduated from college three years ago. She enjoys some parts of her job, but she's being given more and more work to do for no extra money. She often has to do unpaid overtime. After considering it for a while, she finally found the courage to ask her boss for a raise, but she immediately said no. She's stressed and frustrated and doesn't know what to do. She'd like to move to a different company, but she doesn't know of any current vacancies for someone with her skills and experience.

2 Listen to Student A describe Shinji's situation. Offer advice.

3 Imagine you are Olivia. Explain your problem to Student A, using the prompts in the box. Listen to Student A's advice and decide on the best thing to do.

> I'd rather …   If only …   It's about time …   I wish …

10A Student B

1 Read about two human behaviors. Think about how you can use the prompts below each text to tell Student A about each behavior.

Why do we dream?

Sigmund Freud said our dreams represent the things we really want. Other people say dreams are random and meaningless. Actually, dreams are what happen as our brain is organizing all the things that happened during the day. Our dreams are all our memories, and the brain is deciding which memories to keep and which memories to throw away.

> According to …   Apparently …   Dreams are believed …

Why do we make art?

We can communicate most things through language, but not everything. There are certain concepts like love, pain, and beauty that we cannot express through words. Art allows us to more accurately share with people what is happening inside our minds. It also helps us explore our sense of self.

> According to …   It is suggested that …   It seems …

148

COMMUNICATION PRACTICE

2 Listen to Student A answer questions 1–2. Which answer do you find most interesting or surprising?

1 Why do we blush?

2 Why do we laugh?

3 Tell Student A about the two behaviors you read about in exercise 1, using the prompts.

10C Student B

1 Look at the picture and read the story behind it. Note the use of adverbs.

HAPPY BIRTHDAY!

In May 2015, in Sheffield, England, Winnie Blagden was about to turn 100. But the staff at the nursing home where Winnie lived was anxious about her upcoming celebration. Winnie had no family, and the staff thought it was highly improbable that she'd have any visitors. They were also worried that she would receive hardly any cards on her birthday. As a solution, they contacted a local radio station, who agreed it would be incredibly sad if Winnie didn't have a big birthday celebration. So the station organized a social media campaign, asking people to send birthday cards immediately to the nursing home. The campaign was highly successful, and Winnie ended up receiving over 16,000 cards from as far away as Japan and Australia!

2 Look at Student A's picture and listen to the story behind it.

3 Cover the text and tell Student A the story behind your picture. Use adverbs. Which story most restores your faith in humanity?

Phrasal verbs

Phrasal verb	Meaning
back up sb/sth	support sb; save sth
break down	stop working
break out	start suddenly (war, fire, disease)
break up	end a relationship
burn out	become exhausted through overwork
call off sth	cancel
carry out	conduct an experiment (plan)
catch on	become popular
catch up (on sth)	get information; do sth there wasn't time for
cheer up (sb)	make happier
come across	find; seem
come back (to sth)	return (to sth)
come together	join
come up	arise (an issue)
come up with	invent
deal with sth	take action; accept sth
do without sth	manage without
drift apart	separate without actively trying to
figure out sth	understand with careful thought
fit in	be socially compatible (in harmony with)
get along with	have a good relationship
get out of (doing sth)	avoid doing sth
give away sth	give something no longer needed
give in	surrender
go back (a long way)	return; know each other a long time
go through sth	experience sth difficult
grow up	spend one's childhood
hang out	spend time together
hang up	end a phone call
hang sth up	put sth on a hook (hanger)
have sb over	invite sb to your house
hit (it) off	get along very well
hold sb back	prevent sb from moving ahead (succeeding)
let sb down	disappoint

Phrasal verb	Meaning
live up to	fulfill
look down on sb	think one is better or more important
look forward to sth	anticipate; be happy about
look out for sb	watch (protect)
look up to sb	admire (respect)
make up	become friendly after an argument
mess up sth	spoil (do sth badly)
miss out	lose an opportunity
note down sth	write sth to not forget it
pay sb back	repay a loan
pay off	be worthwhile
put up with sth	accept without complaining
reach out (to sb)	contact; show interest in
run out of sth	not have enough
sell out	sell the last one and have no more of
set up sth	establish; prepare for use
settle down	make a home with sb
show up	appear
stand out	be better; be easy to see
talk sb into	convince (persuade)
take after sb	be similar to a family member
take care of	watch (keep safe)
take off	not go to work; succeed
tell sb off	reprimand (scold)
think over sth	consider
think up sth	invent; think of a new idea
throw out	discard (get rid of)
try out sth	use sth to see if you like it
turn up	appear
turn up sth	raise (the volume)
turn down sth	lower (the volume); refuse
turn out	happen (have a certain result)
use up sth	finish (use completely)
work out	exercise; end successfully

IRREGULAR VERBS

Irregular verbs

Infinitive	Simple past	Past participle
arise	arose	arisen
awake	awoke	awoken
bear	bore	born
beat	beat	beaten
bend	bent	beaten
bet	bet	bet
bleed	bled	bled
blow	blew	blown
broadcast	broadcast	broadcast
burn	burned	burned/burnt
burst	burst	burst
catch	caught	caught
creep	crept	crept
cut	cut	cut
deal	dealt	dealt
dig	dug	dug
feed	fed	fed
fight	fought	fought
flee	fled	fled
forbid	forbade	forbidden
forecast	forecast	forecast
forgive	forgave	forgiven
freeze	froze	frozen
hang	hung	hung
hit	hit	hit
hurt	hurt	hurt
kneel	knelt/kneeled	knelt/kneeled
lead	led	led
lean	leaned	leaned
leap	leaped/leapt	leaped/leapt
lend	lent	lent
mean	meant	meant
mistake	mistook	mistaken

Infinitive	Simple past	Past participle
overhear	overheard	overheard
oversleep	overslept	overslept
seek	sought	sought
set	set	set
shake	shook	shaken
shine	shone/shined	shone/shined
shoot	shot	shot
show	showed	shown
shrink	shrank	shrunk
shut	shut	shut
sink	sank	sunk
sleep	slept	slept
slide	slid	slid
smell	smelled	smelled
spin	spun	spun
split	split	split
spill	spilled	spilled/spilt
spoil	spoiled	spoiled
spread	spread	spread
spring	sprang	sprung
stick	stuck	stuck
sting	stung	stung
strike	struck	struck
swear	swore	sworn
sweep	swept	swept
tread	trod	trodden
undertake	undertook	undertaken
undo	undid	undone
upset	upset	upset
weep	wept	wept
wind	wound	wound
withdraw	withdrew	withdrawn
withstand	withstood	withstood

American English

Personal Best

Workbook   **C1** Advanced

UNIT 6 A sense of community

6A LANGUAGE

GRAMMAR: The passive

1 Choose the correct options to complete the sentences.

1 I remember the shock of _____ I would never work again.
 a telling b to be told c being told
2 Marie was very popular. She _____ by all her students.
 a got loved b was loved c loved
3 Your hair looks great! Where _____?
 a did you get it done b was it done
 c did you do it
4 I can't come for you until eleven o'clock. Do you mind _____ a little later?
 a get picked up b be picked up
 c being picked up
5 The boys were throwing a ball around, and somehow a vase _____.
 a got broken b got broke c was broke
6 I had a blood test. I'm waiting _____ the results.
 a telling b being told c to be told
7 It's going to be a great party. I hope _____ on the guest list.
 a being included b to be included
 c to be including
8 Our classroom _____ at the time, so we couldn't go in.
 a was cleaning b had been cleaning
 c was being cleaned

2 Complete the sentences with the correct form of the verbs in parentheses, plus a verb from the box.

| break   wake   call   fix   fire |
| promote   yell   report |

1 Some glasses _____ during the party, and there were bits of glass all over the floor. (get)
2 The incident _____ in the national press last week. (be)
3 My youngest daughter really hates _____ at by the teacher. (get)
4 Ed's already a manager. He _____ twice since he joined the company. (be)
5 I don't know if she'll get the job, but she's likely _____ for an interview. (be)
6 Unfortunately, Alice is unemployed. She _____ from her job last month. (get)
7 I had a terrible night's sleep. I kept _____ up by various people yelling in the street. (be)
8 When her laptop crashed, she _____ it _____ by a friend of your sister's. (get)

VOCABULARY: Neighbors and community

3 Fill in the blanks in the sentences using the anagrams in parentheses to help you.

1 When we moved here, we joined the local community _____. (sascotianoi)
2 After the fire, the whole community came _____ to help rebuild the school. (egothert)
3 Some of the people on this block are renting, but others are _____. (moehwoners)
4 My neighbors always stop and chat, and this gives me a real sense of _____. (lengobing)
5 Events such as summer fairs are a chance for the school to _____ out to the local community. (cerah)
6 The block party gave us the opportunity to meet the _____ from the other apartments. (snetnat)
7 The President has expressed a desire to strengthen _____ between the two countries. (ites)

4 Complete the phrases in the sentences with one word.

1 We're not on a first-name _____ with any of our teachers. They're "Mr. Brown," "Ms. Sylva," and so on.
2 We like to keep an _____ on our elderly neighbors and check that they're OK.
3 This is a very close-_____ community. Everyone knows everyone else.
4 We hadn't met anyone at the party before, so Dan made a funny comment just to _____ the ice.
5 Even though they're both grown up now, Joe is always _____ out for his younger sister and making sure she's OK.
6 People here are very involved in each other's lives. There's a real _____ of community.
7 It's nice to lend a helping _____ to others during difficult times.

PRONUNCIATION: Unstressed have

5 ▶6.1 Listen to the sentences and (circle) the forms of the verb *have* in **bold** when it is unstressed.

1 James **has** just **had** some new curtains made.
2 We **have** recently **had** our windows cleaned.
3 I **had** some shelves built a couple of years ago.
4 Sarah **has had** the ends of her hair dyed pink.
5 They **have had** the old buildings torn down.
6 He **had had** his car serviced before taking off on vacation.

32

SKILLS 6B

LISTENING: Listening for agreement between speakers

1 ▶ 6.2 Listen to a conversation between two people at a party. Notice how they disagree politely with each other. Who do these statements refer to?

1 He/She doesn't know any of his/her neighbors. Daniel / Gabriela
2 He/She spends a lot of time at work. Daniel / Gabriela
3 He/She doesn't want to be involved with the people in his/her community. Daniel / Gabriela
4 At first, he/she didn't know anyone in his/her neighborhood. Daniel / Gabriela
5 He/She enjoyed making friends with his/her neighbors. Daniel / Gabriela
6 He/She doesn't spend many weekends at home. Daniel / Gabriela
7 He/She will probably not move for a long time. Daniel / Gabriela
8 His/Her lifestyle may be different in the future. Daniel / Gabriela

2 ▶ 6.2 Listen to the conversation again. Complete the phrases that the speakers use to agree and politely disagree with each other.

1 Oh, OK. Yeah, _____. I didn't know anyone when I moved into my house …
2 Well, _____. I don't get home till eight o'clock during the week, and on the weekend …
3 _____ it's a shame that you don't even know your neighbors?
4 No, I mean, _____. If you're living somewhere for a while, yes …
5 Yeah, _____. I guess it all depends on what stage of life you're at, doesn't it?

3 ▶ 6.3 Listen again to these sentences from Gabriela and Daniel's conversation. Circle the stressed words in each sentence and underline the unstressed words.

1 What about the neighborhood? Is it friendly?
2 When I've had an exhausting day at the office …
3 I just want to go in and close the door behind me.
4 I'm not sure I'm completely with you on that one.
5 It's really nice to know your neighbors and feel a sense of belonging somewhere, I think.
6 For me, home is just somewhere to eat and sleep.
7 I mean, what if you suddenly needed their help or something?
8 I'm sure I won't live like this forever.

4 Fill in the blanks in the word pairs in the sentences.

1 We've just moved into this apartment, so things are a bit disorganized. We're getting it in order bit by _____, though.
2 Like any adventure, it's had its highs and _____, but we're really pleased we did it.
3 I know lots of people who are crazy about chocolate but, personally, I can take it or _____ it.
4 I'm pleased to say that Isabelle and Clara got back from their travels safe and _____.
5 If I were you, I'd speak to Charles one to _____, rather than raising the issue in a group meeting.
6 Time after _____, we've planned to get together, and every time, Guy has canceled at the last minute.
7 There's no simple solution to the problem. It's just not a black-and-_____ issue.
8 I know we're all very busy, so we'll keep this meeting short and _____.
9 As a director, he was such an important figure in Hollywood that he could make or _____ a young actor.
10 There's a bit of give and _____ in any partnership.

6C LANGUAGE

GRAMMAR: Using linkers

1 Choose the correct options to complete the sentences.

1 We all enjoyed ourselves *even though / despite* it was raining.
2 She drove *as a result / as* it was too far to walk.
3 *Whereas / Unlike* you, I'm not comfortable eating out on my own.
4 They both seemed perfectly cheerful *in spite of / although* all their problems.
5 He retired later that year *because / due to* he was in poor health.
6 Rachel decided to decline the offer *nevertheless / although* she was tempted.
7 Matthew's behavior has been much better this semester. *Although / However*, he still needs to improve.
8 *Because of / As a result* the demonstration in town, both streets were closed.

2 Are these sentences correct or incorrect? Re-write the incorrect sentences.

1 We've had our disagreements over the years, nevertheless I wish her well.
   _____
   _____
2 He never has any money despite he has two jobs.
   _____
   _____
3 As a result the shortage of fresh vegetables, we've had to use other ingredients.
   _____
   _____
4 Whereas teaching focuses on knowledge, training emphasizes skills.
   _____
   _____
5 Unlike my friends, I'm not a huge fan of going to clubs.
   _____
   _____
6 In spite of I had a cold, I enjoyed the evening.
   _____
   _____
7 Our financial position has improved, however we are still not making a profit.
   _____
   _____
8 We're currently expanding our company; consequently, we're advertising for new staff.
   _____
   _____

3 Complete sentences 1–8 with linkers a–h.

1 Astonishingly, Oliver still wasn't full ____ that he'd eaten two plates of food. ____
2 ____ you, I love hot weather. I know you prefer it cooler. ____
3 Neither of us really likes classical music. ____, we went to the concert to support Naomi. ____
4 We really like living in this neighborhood ____ the noise and all the garbage. ____
5 Several streets in the area have been closed ____ the recent bad weather. ____
6 Let the food cool down ____ you'll burn your mouth! ____
7 ____ Jonas loves reading and studying, his twin likes sports and physical activities. ____
8 I crept quietly up the stairs ____ disturb her. ____

a whereas   e or
b so as not to   f nevertheless
c unlike   g as a result of
d despite the fact h despite

4 Complete the sentences with the words in the box.

| so as not to | in spite of | however | since |
| in order to | due to | so that | therefore |

1 I'd assumed you weren't coming to the party _____ you hadn't replied.
2 In some cities, shows have even been canceled _____ the lack of ticket sales.
3 We've had one or two problems along the way. _____, we have made some progress.
4 We are often asked the same questions regarding our products. _____, we have decided to include a list of frequently asked questions.
5 You need to leave in plenty of time _____ you get there for lunch.
6 We've had to make some changes to the service _____ keep costs down.
7 Sylvie's had some personal problems to deal with this year. _____ this, she's managed to achieve all her goals.
8 I was very careful about what I said to Grace _____ offend her.

PRONUNCIATION: Intonation in contrast clauses

5 ▶ 6.4 Listen to the sentences. Pay attention to the rising intonation of the first (contrast) clause. Listen and repeat.

1 Although I like my work, I love going away.
2 Despite the initial problems, the day was a success.
3 In spite of my fatigue, I enjoyed the evening.
4 While my job is pretty stressful, I do enjoy it.
5 Even though the weather wasn't great, we still enjoyed our stay.

34

SKILLS 6D

WRITING: Writing a proposal

1 Read this proposal from Joe Taylor, a member of the Green Road Winter Fair committee, and match headings A–D with blanks 1–4.

A Recommendations   C Introduction
B Conclusion   D Current situation

1 _____

The aim of this proposal is to enable the Winter Fair, a celebration of our vibrant, multicultural community, to take place along Elm Street without interference or danger from vehicles. We are concerned that without traffic restrictions, it will be impossible, in the future, to hold this extremely worthwhile event, which grows in popularity year after year.

2 _____

The fair takes place annually on the first Saturday in December, from 10 a.m. to 5 p.m. It is one of the highlights on our social calendar and has been held for two years. The first year (2017), it was estimated that approximately two hundred people attended the fair. The number doubled in 2018, and we have reason to believe that many more will attend this year. Traffic flow was tolerable, if not ideal, with these relatively small numbers. However, we believe that, going forward, the predicted increase in the number of visitors will make the fair impossible to hold unless there is a change in the current set-up.

3 _____

Our first recommendation would be to close Elm Street to vehicles (including bicycles) between the hours of 9 a.m. and 6 p.m. (The extra time before and after the event would be sufficient for participants to set up and take down their stalls safely.) Specifically, we would like the street closed between Windsor Street and Jackson Street, allowing vehicles to use only the southern part of Elm Street that is not used during the fair.

We would also like to request the closure of White Street Parking to allow us to create an area specifically for selling food. In previous years, food stalls have been located all along Elm Street, wherever a space was available. This set-up gave rise to two problems, littering along Elm Street and obstruction by pedestrians. A dedicated "food fair" would provide an excellent solution to these problems. (It might even be worth closing the parking lot the evening before the fair.)

4 _____

We understand that these recommendations would require considerable organization and expense to implement. However, we would urge you to consider the value of this event to this part of the city, not only in terms of the community spirit that it generates, but also the very considerable extra income it brings to local businesses.

2 Find the formal expressions in the proposal that mean the same as these words and phrases.

1 went to (section 2) _____
2 acceptable, though not very good (section 2) _____
3 in the future (section 2) _____
4 enough (section 3) _____
5 placed in a particular position (section 3) _____
6 caused (section 3) _____
7 start to use (a plan) (section 4) _____
8 advise strongly (section 4) _____

3 Match the sentences from other proposals below (1–6) with the sections (a–d) that they are from.

1 It would be advisable to raise the prices of these products. ___
2 Currently, we have twelve members of staff. ___
3 The aim of this proposal is to protect the population of local sea birds. ___
4 A possible course of action would be to charge the public to use this service. ___
5 We have no doubt about the benefits of the proposal outlined above and ask you to consider it. ___
6 We would also strongly advise consulting local people on the matter. ___

a Introduction   c Recommendations
b Current situation d Conclusion

4 Complete these recommendations with your own ideas.

1 The software in use at present is slightly outdated. It might be worth _____
_____

2 Training was last offered three years ago. It would be advisable _____
_____.

3 The current center is not accessible by public transportation. Our suggestion would be _____
_____.

4 We suggest that you provide a greater variety of hot and cold snacks. We also suggest that _____
_____.

5 Some members of staff seemed unprepared for the changes. We strongly recommend _____
_____.

5 Imagine you have one of these problems in your neighborhood. Write a proposal from your residents' association to city hall suggesting a course of action. Your proposal should be organized into the paragraph types mentioned in exercise 2, use "softened" recommendations, and appropriate formal language.

• an increase in vandalism   • poor street lighting at night
• more burglaries in the   • too much noise at night
  area

35

6 REVIEW and PRACTICE

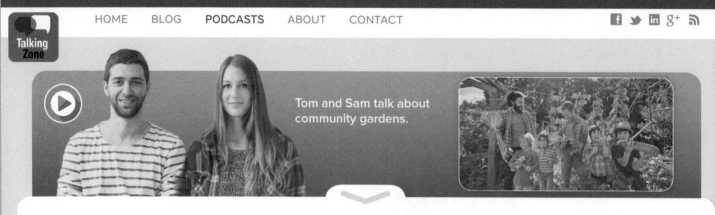

LISTENING

1 ▶ 6.5 Listen to the podcast and number a–f in the order that you hear them (1–6).

a where you can find community gardens ____
b how community gardens became popular in the 1960s ____
c where Tom lives ____
d one use of a community garden involving art ____
e how community gardens help you get to know your neighbors ____
f an explanation of what a community garden is ____

2 ▶ 6.5 Listen again and choose the correct options to complete the sentences.

1 Tom doesn't do any gardening because
   a it doesn't interest him.
   b he doesn't have a garden.
   c he doesn't have any spare time.
2 The best thing about community gardens is that
   a they bring communities together.
   b they provide food for communities.
   c children can gather there.
3 The main purpose of the gardening in these places is to
   a improve people's gardening skills.
   b produce a lot of fruit and vegetables.
   c provide an activity that people can do together.
4 The previous Saturday, children came to the community garden to
   a have a party.
   b learn about plants and animals.
   c draw pictures.
5 Starting in the 1960s, community gardens helped
   a people feel part of their community.
   b feed people in urban neighborhoods.
   c neighbors to get to know each other.
6 Community gardens are found
   a in a variety of places.
   b only in urban areas.
   c usually in schoolyards.

READING

1 Read Tom's blog on page 37 and choose the best summary.

a Tom is pleased that his cousin, Klaas, has finally found housing that he likes, living in a home for elderly people. Previously, Klaas had lived with people his own age, but found that he could not get along with them. Tom thinks he might want to try living like this, too.
b Tom has recently returned from a visit to the Netherlands to see his cousin Klaas, who lives in a home for elderly people. Klaas lives in the home free of charge on the condition that he helps out. The arrangement seems to work well.
c Tom's cousin, Klaas, has a job teaching computer skills to elderly people. One of the benefits of the job is free housing. Klaas likes the people he lives with and chooses to socialize with them, rather than people of his own age.

2 Are the sentences true (T), false (F), or doesn't say (DS)?

1 Tom usually posts about things that bring enjoyment and pleasure. ____
2 Tom often takes vacations in the Netherlands. ____
3 Klaas is the only young person living in the complex. ____
4 He shares his apartment with some elderly people. ____
5 He has more money than he used to have. ____
6 Klaas can decide how many hours he wants to work at the home. ____
7 Klaas's duties involve providing both company and practical help. ____
8 All of the residents love the food that Klaas cooks. ____
9 Klaas gets along very well with his elderly neighbors. ____
10 Tom wishes his grandparents lived in a home like the one Klass lives in. ____

REVIEW and PRACTICE 6

HOME BLOG PODCASTS ABOUT CONTACT

This week Tom writes about his cousin's unusual living arrangement.

Bridging the generation gap

Readers of this blog know that I like the fun things in life. (I have to admit, I'm rarely accused of being too serious.) So I realize the tone of this post might be a little different from previous ones, but please don't let that put you off from reading it.

You see, I've just come back from a trip to the Netherlands to see Klaas, my super-cool Dutch cousin. Klaas, 20, is into music (especially rap), vegan food, and body art. He's possibly the best street dancer I've ever seen. And he lives in a home for the elderly.

Or, at least, he lives in an apartment that's part of a bigger complex where elderly people live. And, in return for being a good neighbor 25 hours a week, Klaas gets to live there absolutely free. So how does this arrangement work? Well, *incredibly well*. Klaas is happier than I've ever seen him (not to mention better off!). For 25 hours a week, he socializes with the residents, telling them about his girlfriend or his studies, and showing off his latest dance moves. And, in addition to providing his neighbors with conversation and laughter, Klaas keeps an eye on them. If people need help tying their shoes or finding their canes, he's there to lend a helping hand. Everyone seems to love him. As one resident explained, before Klaas joined their community, she rarely got to see young people. For years now, even before she went into the home, she'd been largely ignored by people under 30. Now, she spends a large portion of each day in the company of a young person. And, despite the fact that she seems to have nothing in common with my tattooed, rap-loving cousin, they clearly find a lot to talk about!

I joined Klaas in one of his computer sessions where he was teaching his neighbors how to use the Internet. I was amazed to see my *extremely* energetic, party-boy cousin calmly taking his neighbors through the steps needed to Google local restaurants and coffee shops. Later, I watched him cooking with his neighbors and, although one or two of them seemed a little doubtful about Klaas's vegan stew, they were all persuaded to try it.

Later that evening, I asked Klaas what he got out of his unusual living arrangement, and his answer surprised me. He was enjoying all the contact with his neighbors. According to him, they were more sociable than anyone he'd previously lived with, coming together regularly in order to cook, exercise, and watch television. Whereas Klaas had previously only socialized in the evening, he was now mixing with people at various points throughout the day. He liked living in a place that had a real sense of community.

Overall, I was very struck by how successful this arrangement was and wondered if our own approach to housing is sometimes a little unimaginative. What do you think?

Modern life

GRAMMAR: Verb patterns (2): reporting

1 Choose the correct options to complete the sentences.

1 They threatened to *call / calling / called* the police.
2 She walked into the room and announced that she *left / was leaving / had left*.
3 He told me that he *will / would / wouldn't* accompany me if I wanted him to.
4 My boss asked me why *I haven't / hadn't I / I hadn't* finished the work on time.
5 Marie mentioned that she *was finding / had found / has found* a passport in the street.
6 Al asked me what *I thought / I'm thinking / did I think* of his new haircut.
7 Paul insists that we *deleted / have deleted / delete* any photos of him immediately.
8 His parents begged him *being / had been / to be* careful.

2 Complete the reported version of each sentence.

1 "I've read all his novels."
   She claimed that _____ all his novels.
2 "My dad can give Max a ride to the station."
   She said _____ Max a ride to the station.
3 "I'll definitely help with the cooking."
   He promised _____ with the cooking.
4 "I think he should see a specialist."
   She recommended that _____ a specialist.
5 "What are you eating?"
   He asked me _____ .
6 "Perhaps you could take French lessons."
   She suggested that _____ French lessons.
7 "The vacation won't be as much fun without Laura."
   He said the vacation _____ as much fun without Laura.
8 "I altered the figures on the document."
   She admitted _____ the figures on the document.

VOCABULARY: Technology

3 Complete the sentences with the words and phrases in the box.

| crash   bandwidth   wireless network   computer-literate |
| unplug   work remotely   bug   charge the battery |

1 I don't have a desk at work because I usually _____ .
2 The programmer had to fix a _____ in the software.
3 You can plug your phone into my laptop to _____ .
4 We don't have enough _____ to stream the video live.
5 This password allows me to access the company's _____ .
6 They're worried that high demand for the product could cause their website to _____ .
7 You need to be extremely _____ to do this job.
8 Please remember to _____ all electronic equipment before leaving the building.

4 Read the definitions and complete the words.

1 a document or picture that you send with an e-mail or a text = a_____
2 an arrow that moves around a computer screen to show where you are = c_____
3 a system that enables your computer to send and receive large amounts of data = b_____
4 a program that lets you access the Internet = b_____
5 start to use a computer system, by typing your name and/or password = l_____ i_____
6 move your finger across a touchscreen to activate a function = s_____
7 put a piece of software on your computer = i_____
8 a general word for any computer, smartphone, tablet, etc. = d_____
9 disconnect a piece of equipment from its source of electricity = u_____
10 move to or towards the top of a piece of text or an image on a computer screen = s_____ u_____

PRONUNCIATION: Consonant clusters

5 ▶ 7.1 Read these sentences aloud, paying attention to the consonant clusters. Can you hear the sounds in **bold** in the underlined words? Listen and repeat.

1 My mother tol**d** me to be home by ten.
2 She as**k**ed the man for directions to the station.
3 The man beg**g**ed me to give him some food.
4 She still insi**s**ts that she is innocent.
5 He encourage**d** me to become more independent.
6 She usually as**k**s Tom to help her.

SKILLS 7B

READING: Understanding the writer's purpose

Living alone: is this the new normal?

Throughout history, people have formed families or family-like groups, but ¹it appears that this may be changing. Startling statistics indicate that the number of people living alone is skyrocketing, especially in the metropolitan cities of the world's richer nations. In the old days, ²it was common to marry young and remain with your spouse until death. Nowadays, people are marrying later and divorcing more frequently, often spending many years alone between marriages or not remarrying at all.

In 2016, around 35.25 million people in the U.S. and 7.7 million in the U.K. lived in single-occupancy households, and ³it is thought that this upward trend will continue. However, solitary living is far from simply the unintended, and unwanted, consequence of family breakdown. On the contrary, ⁴it is becoming an increasingly common lifestyle choice. Real-estate agents report that many young people who might previously have opted to share an apartment are now looking to live on their own.

Some sociologists believe ⁵it is modern society's demand for constant connection that has led to the increase in the number of people seeking solitude at home. Many people report a huge sense of relief at being able to relax on their own at the end of a work day, as well as the pleasure they get from being free to please only themselves. Apparently, where solitary confinement was once seen as a punishment, ⁶it is now considered desirable!

We have also seen the growing phenomenon of LAT (Living Apart Together) couples – people in committed relationships who nevertheless choose to maintain their individual living arrangements. Some claim that living apart helps prevent their relationship from becoming monotonous. This is because while couples living separately tend to make more of an effort to engage in interesting activities together, ⁷it is easy for couples that live together to fall into a routine, which can cause the relationship to become stale. Since LAT couples have to plan their time together, they are more likely to continue to make an effort to ensure that ⁸it remains both interesting and successful.

Living alone can certainly have downsides. The financial burden of not having anyone to share bills with is very real, and nobody should underestimate the isolation that some single people suffer from. But for those who value their privacy and independence, ⁹it can be extremely rewarding, providing the time and space for both relaxation and self-development, not to mention freedom from arguments about housework!

1 Choose the correct options to complete the sentences.

1 The number of single-occupancy households is
  a forecast to double.
  b increasing rapidly.
  c only happening in cities.
2 One reason more people are living alone is that
  a marriages are shorter.
  b fewer people get married.
  c more people are living longer.
3 Young adults often live alone because
  a they can only afford small apartments.
  b they prefer to do so.
  c they do not have friends to share with.
4 The desire to live alone may be due to
  a an increase in selfishness.
  b a modern idea that living alone is a good thing.
  c too much communication in our daily lives.
5 Couples who live apart
  a have to make a lot of effort, or, otherwise, their relationships will fail.
  b do more activities than those who live together.
  c are less likely to become bored in their relationships.
6 People who live alone face extra expenses because
  a they have to pay for all the costs of running a household by themselves.
  b they often live in remote places and have higher transportation costs.
  c housing for a single person is more expensive.

2 The sentences below come from a variety of different texts. Match sentences 1–8 with the purpose of the text from which they have been taken (a–d).

1 A new city hall could potentially benefit every single member of our community. ____
2 Buses run every half hour from the central train station. ____
3 The piece of ham slipped out of her sandwich and lay unnoticed on her lap. ____
4 Take two of these pills three times a day with meals. ____
5 He was wearing an enormous pair of star-shaped sunglasses and a tall, pointed hat. ____
6 Risso's dolphins usually live in deep, tropical waters. ____
7 When playing this passage, do not lift the bow from the string. ____
8 Turning the heat down by just one degree could save 10% on your energy bills. ____

a to inform   c to instruct
b to persuade   d to entertain

3 Look at the underlined uses of *it* in the text. Write P when it is used as a pronoun and G when it has a grammatical use. Which word or idea does *it* refer to when it is used as a pronoun?

1 ____   4 ____   7 ____
2 ____   5 ____   8 ____
3 ____   6 ____   9 ____

39

7C LANGUAGE

GRAMMAR: Future time

1 Complete the sentences with the words in the box.

> will be broadcasting   will have broadcast
> were going to search   will have been searching
> was broadcasting   will have searched
> will be searching   will have been broadcasting

1 The police _____ all the rooms by 4 p.m.
2 I knew the channel _____ the show later that week.
3 On May 2nd, police _____ for the missing boy for a year.
4 They _____ the loft, but in the end, there was no time.
5 By the time she returns from her trip tomorrow, they _____ the interview.
6 Next year, Radio X _____ for 50 years!
7 The police say they _____ the area tomorrow.
8 On their website, it says they _____ the show later this year.

2 Are the underlined future forms in the conversation correct or incorrect? Cross out any mistakes and write the correct verb forms above them. Use only the future continuous, future perfect, future perfect continuous, or forms that show the future in the past.

A Have you been at this company for long?
B Yes, ¹I'll have been working here for ten years next month.
A Really? ²Will you have done anything special to celebrate?
B Yes, but nothing big. ³I'll just have invited a few of my colleagues for a drink.
A So you enjoy it here, then?
B Most of the time. ⁴I was thinking of leaving a while back. ⁵I'll have been retraining as a physiotherapist. But then I got a promotion, and the company offered to pay for me to take a course in accounting.
A And have you completed it now?
B Not quite. ⁶I'll have finished the course in December, as long as I pass! And you? Are you happy working here?
A It's OK, but ⁷I won't have stayed for ten years, that's for sure, because I really want to work in the U.K. ⁸I'll be going last year, but my sister had a baby, and I wanted to stay and help her for a while. ⁹I'll have been looking for another job soon, though, because ¹⁰I'll have been living in this city for five years soon, and that's too long in one place for me!

VOCABULARY: Expressions with *world* and *place*

3 Choose the correct options.

1 If you **think the world of** someone, you
   a believe that he/she is extremely important.
   b like or love him/her very much.
   c would do anything to be with him/her.
2 Something that is **all over the place** is
   a hard to gather together.
   b extremely common.
   c done in a careless and unsatisfactory way.
3 Something that is **out of this world**
   a is extremely good.
   b does not exist in real life.
   c is very far away.
4 If two things are **worlds apart**,
   a they are very far away from one another.
   b they are totally different from one another.
   c one is much better than the other.
5 Someone who is **in first place**
   a is winning a race or competition.
   b is older than the others in a group.
   c gets the best grades on in an exam.

4 Complete the sentences with the missing words.

1 Once we had the funding, everything else _____ place pretty quickly, and the business was successful soon.
2 It turns out that my neighbor is a friend of my cousin – _____ world, isn't it?
3 There are lots of reasons to get exercise. _____ place, it makes you feel happier.
4 Max wasn't available, so the meeting _____ place without him.
5 I know you're upset that you didn't win the contract, but it's _____ world. We already have plenty of work.

PRONUNCIATION: Unstressed words in future forms

5 ▶ 7.2 Read the sentences aloud and then decide whether the underlined words are stressed (S) or unstressed (U). Listen and check.

		S	U
1	She was traveling to Mexico later that day.	___	___
2	I will have gotten my test results by then.	___	___
3	They were going to pay the money back the following week.	___	___
4	They'll have been waiting for more than an hour.	___	___
5	He'll be living in France next year.	___	___

SKILLS 7D

SPEAKING: Disagreeing tactfully

1 ▶ 7.3 Listen to Anna and Lori discussing whether to rent out their spare room. Fill in the blanks in these sentences from their conversation.

1 I'm not _____ about that. The apartment's not very big.
2 I take your _____, but _____ I see it, we could work something out.
3 I'm afraid I _____ it _____. I think it could be awkward.
4 That's a _____, but just think of all the things we could do with the extra cash!
5 But **then** _____, it's great having the apartment to ourselves, too.
6 _____ **hand**, I do agree that a bit more money would be nice.
7 Well, **another way of** _____ **is** that it would give us a chance to meet interesting people from all over the world.

2 Match functions a–c to the phrases in **bold** (1–7) used by Anna and Lori in exercise 1.

a disagree using tentative language   ____ ____
b introduce an opposite opinion   ____ ____
c acknowledge the other person's opinion   ____ ____

3 Charlie and Lois are discussing the benefits of going to college. Complete their conversation with the phrases in the box. There may be more than one correct answer.

> I'm not sure I see it the same way.   On the other hand, …
> I'm not sure I agree.   Another point of view is …
> I see where you're coming from, but …

Charlie If you don't go to college, you'll never get a good job.
Lois ¹_____. There are lots of successful businesspeople who didn't go to college. And what about all those students majoring in subjects like art history or media studies? That's just a waste of time when it comes to having a good career.
Charlie ²_____. In my opinion, the experience of studying is a useful one in itself. It teaches you a lot about thinking skills and analyzing evidence.
Lois ³_____ those are very abstract skills. ⁴_____ that it's better to learn a skill in the real world. If you're going to be, say, an electrician, which is a good job, you just need to start work as an apprentice. ⁵_____, I admit I wouldn't want a doctor who hadn't been to college!

4 Write two short conversations, using the prompts below.

1 Ben and Ethan are trying to decide where to go on vacation:
Ben [suggest an option] _____
Ethan [disagree tentatively] _____
Ben [ask Ethan to make a suggestion] _____
Ethan [suggest an option] _____
Ben [suggest a compromise solution] _____

2 Katie and Ella are discussing whether to buy a new couch:
Katie [state the advantages of buying a new couch] _____
Ella [acknowledge Katie's opinion but then introduce an opposite opinion] _____
Katie [disagree tentatively] _____
Ella [suggest some areas of common agreement] _____
Katie [give an opinion about the best option] _____

41

7 REVIEW and PRACTICE

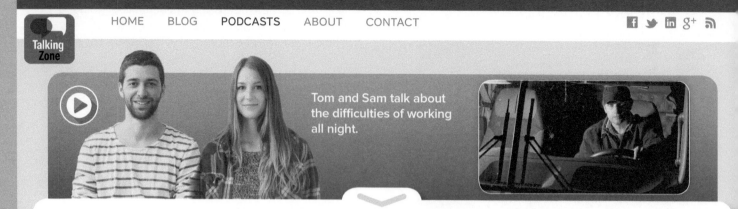

HOME   BLOG   **PODCASTS**   ABOUT   CONTACT

Tom and Sam talk about the difficulties of working all night.

LISTENING

1 ▶ 7.4 Listen to the conversation and give short answers to the following questions.

1. How long will Tom and Sam have to stay awake for their charity broadcast? _____
2. What is Graham's job? _____
3. What is Jenny's job? _____
4. Who complained about Jenny working nights? _____
5. What were Graham and his wife celebrating at the restaurant? _____

2 ▶ 7.4 Listen again. Who said the following things? Write T for Tom, S for Sam, G for Graham, J for Jenny, or N for Nobody.

1. He/She is bad-tempered when he/she doesn't sleep enough. ____
2. He/She wants advice about staying up all night. ____
3. They're doing a charity broadcast with a couple of other people. ____
4. It's better to do his/her job at night than during the day. ____
5. He/She is in good shape and healthy at the moment. ____
6. He/She wants to stop working at night in the future. ____
7. He/She always finds it very easy to get to sleep. ____
8. Working at night affects his/her social life. ____
9. He/She doesn't go to nice restaurants often. ____
10. It's easier to stay awake if you're hungry. ____

READING

1 Read Tom's blog on page 43 and number a–f in the order that he mentions them.

a. forgetting to make a copy of some work ____
b. his grandmother's home ____
c. his overall opinion of computers ____
d. forgetting to send an image with an e-mail ____
e. an event that was spoiled by a technological error ____
f. sending an e-mail to the wrong people ____

2 Are the following statements true (T), false (F), or doesn't say (DS)?

1. Tom likes his grandmother very much. ____
2. It's not possible to get broadband where she lives. ____
3. Tom doesn't mind not being able to use his cell phone or laptop next week. ____
4. His grandmother wishes she had good cell-phone signal. ____
5. Tom isn't always good at using technology. ____
6. His mom was sympathetic when he lost his schoolwork. ____
7. Tom put a lot of effort into the e-mail to his landlord. ____
8. The landlord didn't correct the problem in the bedroom because Tom forgot to send the photo. ____
9. The software Tom and Sam used for their presentation was easy to use. ____
10. Tom thinks his friends will wonder where he is next week. ____

REVIEW and PRACTICE 7

HOME **BLOG** PODCASTS ABOUT CONTACT

Tom writes about the joys and perils of computers.

The pros and cons of being digitally dependent

I'll be staying with my grandma next week. I think the world of my grandma, and I love spending time in her quaint little home in the country. But there's just one drawback: it's so remote that there's no cell-phone signal, whatsoever, and she doesn't have broadband, which means I'll be completely disconnected for a week! A whole week!

My grandma is totally unsympathetic. In fact, when I mentioned it, she replied sarcastically that it was a miracle she'd managed to survive this long without the Internet. I tried to explain all the cool things she could do if she was computer-literate, but not only was she very skeptical about their value, she also reminded me (rather unkindly, I thought) of several times when technology had let me down badly.

OK, I admit it, my record on this is less than sparkling. Starting with the time when, at the age of 15, I tried to plan a secret party while my parents were away, but somehow managed to copy them in on the message. Since then, my technological mishaps have become something of a family legend. I once lost a whole semester's work because my laptop got stolen, and I hadn't backed it up anywhere. I had to spend my entire vacation redoing it and, what's more, instead of comforting me, my mom said it really wasn't too smart of me to let the laptop out of my sight.

It still hurts to remember the painstakingly crafted e-mail I once sent to my landlord about the damp spots in my bedroom. I was convinced that the attached photo of moldy green walls would prompt both shame at his negligence and immediate action to rectify the problem. Sadly, it was only a couple of days later that I realized I had sent the message without the attachment, and was forced to compose a slightly apologetic follow-up, which rather detracted from my previous words of righteous fury.

However, that was a minor embarrassment compared to the time my laptop crashed right in the middle of a presentation to a major broadcasting company that Sam and I were trying to persuade to fund a series of short films we wanted to make. We'd spent so long preparing state-of-the-art visuals, using some really complex software (it practically had us tearing our hair out at times!), that it was heart-breaking to end up looking so unprofessional.

However, my grandma and I are still worlds apart when it comes to the digital age. She sees computers basically as the root of most of contemporary society's evils, whereas I feel they have brought about enormous advances. I just need to learn to use them a bit better sometimes! Anyway, next week, I'll be living by her rules. I just hope I won't have lost all my online friends by the time I get back!

UNIT 8 Inspire and innovate

8A LANGUAGE

GRAMMAR: Relative clauses with quantifiers and prepositions

1 Complete the sentences with the phrases in the box. There are two that you don't need.

> some of whom   the best of which   none of which
> both of whom   the highest of which
> in which case   the last of which   at which point
> all of whom   by which time

1 Sometimes she feels like a failure because she has three sisters, _____ have far better jobs than her.
2 They didn't get here until 3 p.m., _____ the meal was ruined.
3 We want everyone to write a poem, _____ will be included in the book.
4 We took a group of children, _____ had never been to the countryside before.
5 These are the Himalayan mountains, _____ is Everest.
6 When she saw her wrecked car, she said lots of things, _____ I can repeat!
7 The car may not start, _____ we'll have to take a taxi.
8 He wrote 30 novels, _____ was completed just days before his death.

2 Add one relative pronoun and one preposition to complete each sentence. Write ^ where they should go and add the words above the line. Pay attention to whether the sentence is formal or informal.

1 She misses the husband she was married for over 40 years. (formal)
2 This is the brush I clean my boots. (informal)
3 This is an achievement you can be really proud. (informal)
4 I wrote a detailed report on the issue, I was paid very well. (formal)
5 She is the type of person you can always rely. (formal)
6 That's the store I bought my watch. (informal)
7 It was a situation I had absolutely no control. (formal)
8 Is that the box you put the documents? (informal)

VOCABULARY: Science and discovery

3 Choose the correct options.

1 She came up with several *conclusive / hypothetical / classified* situations to illustrate her point.
2 I do not agree with her *analysis / innovation / evidence* of their strengths and weaknesses.
3 The evidence they presented was far from *proven / conclusive / theoretical*.
4 These hotels are *influenced / theorized / classified* according to price.
5 His stay in Paris was the *theory / inspiration / innovation* for the novel.

4 Complete the second sentence so that it means the same as the first sentence. Use a word from the same family as the underlined word, and any other necessary words.

1 Nobody could prove that he killed her.
   There was no _____ that he killed her.
2 She continues to innovate in her designs.
   She continues to produce _____ designs.
3 She came up with the hypothesis that the objects were Roman.
   She _____ that the objects were Roman.
4 His opinions have a lot of influence in the art world.
   His opinions are very _____ in the art world.
5 Has anybody evaluated the program?
   Has anybody carried out _____ the program?
6 My brother's success has inspired me.
   I find my brother's success _____.
7 I reached the conclusion that her death was suspicious.
   I _____ that her death was suspicious.
8 The different designs were experimental.
   They _____ different designs.

PRONUNCIATION: Sentence stress

5 ▶ 8.1 Read the sentences aloud. Underline the stressed words in the phrases in **bold**. Listen and check.

1 We waited until noon, **at which point** we gave up and went home.
2 The hall was full of people, **all of whom** were there to hear her speak.
3 Is that the car they **came in**?
4 He gave us two photos, **one of which** was damaged.
5 He's the type of man **for whom** I would do anything.

44

SKILLS 8B

LISTENING: Identifying signposting language

1 ▶ 8.2 Listen to Olivia, Bryn, and Clara talking about creativity. Are the following statements true (T), false (F), or doesn't say (DS)?

1. Bryn notices that Olivia is unhappy. ____
2. Olivia has written several novels. ____
3. Bryn makes a lot of money from his inventions. ____
4. Clara writes her best poetry when a relationship ends. ____
5. Olivia wants to break up with her boyfriend. ____
6. Bryn enjoys going to the gym. ____
7. Clara recommends that Olivia go somewhere quiet to write. ____
8. After the conversation, Olivia knows how to finish her novel. ____

2 Complete the conversation with the signposting phrases in the box. Use each phrase once.

> as I've already mentioned   in other words
> where does that lead us   so, to sum up   let's turn to
> and lastly   for starters   let me put it this way

A I think we all have to accept that this theater is in trouble. ¹_____, audiences have been getting smaller. Secondly, reviews have been poor. ²_____, an increasing number of actors are reluctant to work here.

B Will we have to close?

A Well, ³_____: unless we make some fairly radical changes, that's a distinct possibility.

B So, ⁴_____?

A OK, well, we discussed the choice of plays last week, and we've agreed on a new program for the autumn season, so ⁵_____ our marketing. Clearly, people won't come to a play if they don't hear about it. ⁶_____ in previous meetings, I don't feel we're reaching our target audience. ⁷_____, we need to think harder about where we spend our advertising budget.

B ⁸_____, our strategy is to make our plays more popular and target our advertising more effectively.

A Yes, exactly.

3 ▶ 8.3 Read the sentences aloud. Is the underlined sound /tʃ/ or /dʒ/? Listen and check.

	/tʃ/	/dʒ/
1 Shouldn't you be in your English class?	____	____
2 Someone should call her, but not you.	____	____
3 Should your mom know about this?	____	____
4 Haven't you finished your essay yet?	____	____
5 Could you help me with these bags, please?	____	____
6 I found your book under the sofa.	____	____

4 Complete the sentences with the nouns from these phrasal verbs. Check a dictionary for hyphenation.

> take off   back up   catch up
> break up   give away   mix up
> break down   let down

1. This nice beach bag was a _____ from the travel agent.
2. After all the excitement, the party was a bit of a _____.
3. I was late because of a _____ with the travel arrangements.
4. The computer in the room should be fine, but I've brought my laptop as a _____.
5. I asked my designer for a _____ of all the costs.
6. You need to turn your phone off during _____.
7. I never see my friends anymore. We're always playing _____.
8. I moved abroad after a painful _____.

45

8C LANGUAGE

GRAMMAR: Mixed conditionals and alternatives to *if*

1 Are the sentences correct or incorrect?

	Correct	Incorrect
1 You can come on the boat provided you had your own life jacket.	___	___
2 If you hadn't promised to meet Joe, you can stay and eat with us.	___	___
3 Suppose the train is delayed, what will you do?	___	___
4 If she really cared about you, she would have done more to help.	___	___
5 If I hadn't had the operation, I wouldn't have been alive today.	___	___
6 I wouldn't have chosen to study law I had known how hard it was.	___	___
7 I'm definitely going for a run, whether it's raining or not.	___	___
8 You would feel better if you hadn't eaten so much chocolate.	___	___
9 As long as you study hard, you'd pass your exams.	___	___
10 If she'd saved more, she would have retired when she turns 65.	___	___

2 Complete these mixed conditional sentences with the correct form of the verbs in parentheses.

1 If I _____ a bike, I would have ridden into town. (have)
2 If we hadn't gotten lost, we _____ there by now. (be)
3 We would have gone to the Indian restaurant if Ben _____ spicy food so much. (not dislike)
4 If he _____ so many times in the past, we would be more likely to believe him now. (not lie)
5 If I _____ those e-mails, I still wouldn't know about their plans. (not see)
6 She would _____ you more if you hadn't been so rude about her cooking. (like)
7 If Joe hadn't agreed to work all summer, he _____ on vacation with us next month. (come)
8 I _____ the museum more often when I lived in New York if I liked modern art. [visit]

3 Combine the sentences using the words in parentheses. Make any other changes necessary. The first one has been done for you.

1 You can go to the lake. You have to have an adult with you, though. (as long as)
You can go to the lake as long as you have an adult with you.

2 Harry might not let you stay at his apartment. What will you do? (supposing)
_____

3 I'm going to get tickets for the festival. I hope I'll have enough money. (provided)
_____

4 I wish we hadn't gone to see the movie. We didn't know how boring it would be. (had)
_____

5 You may look at the paintings. However, you can't take any photos. (provided)
_____

6 I'm going to New York. I'll still go if you decide not to come with me. (whether or not)
_____

7 It's fine to play music. Please don't have it on too loud, though. (so long as)
_____

8 You should go to bed now. If you don't, you'll be tired tomorrow. (otherwise)
_____

PRONUNCIATION: Weak forms

4 ▶ 8.4 Read the sentences aloud. Are the words in **bold** pronounced with their weak or strong forms? Listen and check.

	Weak	Strong
1 If I **had** remembered my sweater, I wouldn't be so cold.	___	___
2 **Had** we known Chris was coming, we would have stayed longer.	___	___
3 If I was braver, I would **have** gone into the cave.	___	___
4 I would have brought you a present **had** I known it was your birthday.	___	___
5 We'd be better at our jobs if we had **had** more training.	___	___
6 If we'd called her earlier, Mom **would** be here by now.	___	___
7 If they **had** had a better teacher, they would know more French.	___	___
8 If we **had** brought our tennis rackets, we could play.	___	___

SKILLS 8D

WRITING: Opinion and discussion essays

Which college system is best for students: the broader U.S. model or the specialist U.K. model?

A On the other hand, some people feel that the U.S. system is too shallow and results in a relatively superficial level of study. Students in British universities are trained to dive much deeper into a single area. As one history professor put it, in the U.S., he taught his students some history; in the U.K., he was able to teach them to become historians. Particularly in professional subjects such as law or medicine, the U.K. system sets students on their career path earlier.

B Students in the U.S. spend their first year taking a range of courses, only later choosing a "major" subject. In addition, all students continue to take additional, often unrelated, "elective" courses. This flexibility means that students are free to explore new interests and end up with a much broader education. It avoids the situation, common in the U.K., where someone who is highly educated in one subject has almost no knowledge of other essential areas of study.

C To sum up, there are advantages and disadvantages to both systems. For many students who have no fixed career path in mind, the broader U.S. system may work well. It is certainly desirable that an art historian also have a basic knowledge of math and science, or that a physicist be familiar with some of the world's great novels. However, for those who aren't in doubt about their chosen subject, or who wish to work at a deeper, specialized level, the more focused U.K. system may be preferable.

D According to one respected education journal, over half of the world's top 200 colleges are in the U.S. and the U.K. Students come from all over the world, often paying large sums of money for the outstanding education they offer. However, the two systems are very different. In the U.K., undergraduates usually focus on one subject only, favoring depth over breadth, while in the U.S., the opposite is true.

---

1 A Read the essay and number paragraphs A–D in the correct order 1–4.

1 ____   2 ____   3 ____   4 ____

B What sort of essay is it?

a an opinion essay ____
b a discussion essay ____

2 Find the following synonyms in the text:

1 two words that mean "not deep" (paragraph A).
_____, _____

2 two words or phrases that mean "the topics students learn about" (paragraph B).
_____, _____

3 two words that mean "narrow" (paragraph C).
_____, _____

4 two words that mean "those studying in college" (paragraph D). _____, _____

3 Imagine you are writing an essay on the topic below. Complete the sentences using your own ideas.

> **Is college education a waste of time and money for most young people?**
>
> 1 More young people are going to college than ever before. This situation means _____.
>
> 2 Young people need the experience of a real working environment in order to _____.
>
> 3 Although college can be very expensive, _____.
>
> 4 Many graduates are struggling to find suitable employment. Therefore, _____.
>
> 5 Some major companies offer training programs for graduates. Opportunities like this _____.
>
> 6 College teaches much more than simply the subject being studied. For example, _____.

4 Write an essay on the topic in exercise 3. You can choose whether to write an opinion essay or a discussion essay.

- Structure your essay with an introduction, two paragraphs in the main body, and a conclusion.
- Use cohesive devices such as synonyms, reference words, summary nouns, and linking words.

8 REVIEW and PRACTICE

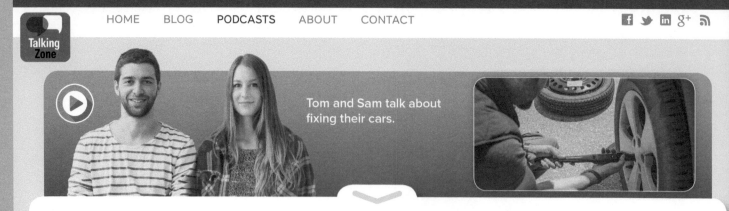

LISTENING

1 ▶ 8.5 Listen to Tom and Sam discussing modern cars. Check (✓) the things they talk about.

1. The cost of modern car repairs. _____
2. The popularity of electric cars. _____
3. The contrast with older cars. _____
4. How people used to take classes in car maintenance. _____
5. Some of the useful features of modern cars. _____
6. The reason you can't buy simple cars nowadays. _____
7. A time that Tom's car broke down. _____
8. A possible future innovation in car tires. _____

2 ▶ 8.5 Listen again and choose the correct options to complete the sentences.

1. Sam's grandpa was able to repair his own car because
   a. he was a good mechanic.
   b. the engine was fairly simple.
   c. most people learned to do it in those days.
2. Tom likes the features modern cars have because
   a. they help him when he has to drive backwards.
   b. they are useful for an experienced driver like him.
   c. he enjoys driving more because of them.
3. Sam believes that car manufacturers
   a. are no longer able to produce simpler cars.
   b. would like to be able to produce simpler cars.
   c. would stop anyone from producing simpler cars.
4. Tom says that his dad's car
   a. broke down less often than his own car.
   b. often used to have problems on trips.
   c. often wouldn't start.
5. When Sam had a flat tire,
   a. it was difficult to get someone to fix it.
   b. she decided to learn how to change a tire herself.
   c. she missed her flight.
6. Sam isn't happy about changing a tire because
   a. she thinks the wheel might come off while she's driving.
   b. she's not strong enough to do it.
   c. she doesn't really understand how to do it.

READING

1 Read Tom's blog on page 49 and choose the best summary.

a. Tom recently spent a day at a center for troubled children. The center offers a range of unusual activities as well as normal classes. The students stay for 10 weeks, but Tom wants to raise money to help them stay for longer.
b. Tom visited a center for young people who haven't been in conventional education in a long time. He observed some of their activities and was so impressed that he wants his readers to donate money to start a similar program at home.
c. Last week Tom went to a place that helps young people gain the confidence to return to school. He was very impressed by the work of the center, particularly the work they do with horses. The center is struggling to keep up its work, so Tom wants his readers to give it money.

2 Check (✓) the things that Tom says.

1. The young people at Parson's Hall have all committed a crime. _____
2. He is convinced that places like Parson's Hall do good work. _____
3. The classes he saw were not like conventional school classes. _____
4. The child with concentration problems enjoys horseback riding. _____
5. The discussion group was given real-life problems to solve. _____
6. The children do not always behave in a calm and mature way. _____
7. The teacher was disappointed by the behavior of the anxious boy. _____
8. Young people who go to Parson's Hall often benefit significantly. _____
9. The letter Tom read was from someone who has friends in jail. _____
10. Tom intends to go back to Parson's Hall to help with its work. _____

REVIEW and PRACTICE 8

HOME   BLOG   PODCASTS   ABOUT   CONTACT

Tom writes about an innovative program for high school dropouts.

A school with a difference

Last week, on a trip to the U.K., I was lucky enough to visit a truly inspirational place on my trip to the U.K., and I'm blogging about it today because I want all of you (yes, you too, Sam!) to dig deep in your pockets to support it.

Parsons Hall, a rambling old house deep in the Devon countryside, in the south of England, provides a temporary home for up to thirty troubled young people that conventional schools have given up on, and, to my mind, offers conclusive proof that many more young people should be given the opportunities it provides.

On the day I visited, the students, none of whom have attended a normal school for at least two years, all seemed to be engaged in some sort of meaningful, if unconventional, learning. One group was working with horses, in a program designed to get them to understand the animals' emotions and relate them to their own. The teacher told me that one child, who had previously been unable to concentrate for more than a couple of minutes at a time, would happily spend over an hour quietly observing the horses and making notes.

In another group, students were given hypothetical problems that required them to discuss and collaborate with each other in order to come up with solutions. The only rule was that everyone's ideas should be treated with respect, whether or not the others thought they were reasonable. For these kids, many of whom have been the victims of bullying, this is the first time they have felt comfortable enough to participate in a group activity and put forward their own ideas.

Of course, a place like this is no miracle cure. I witnessed a few tears and tantrums, as well as one pale young man who sat in silence, slightly shaking, during the entire class that I observed him in. However, the teacher told me afterwards that merely being present in the classroom represented a major breakthrough for him, since at home, his severe anxiety had practically made him a prisoner in his own bedroom.

Students spend ten weeks at Parsons Hall. According to head teacher Michelle Wilson, the experience often has a profound influence on their lives, with many of them going on to participate in conventional education again. A recent independent evaluation of the program also showed significant improvements in the young people's self-esteem and mental health. Michelle showed me a letter from a young woman in which she said that if she hadn't come to Parsons Hall, she would probably be in jail now, like several of her friends.

I've come away inspired! I'd like to start a similar program here at home. So, wallets out now, guys! The address that you should send your contributions to is at the bottom of this post. Please be generous!

UNIT 9 Connections

9A LANGUAGE

GRAMMAR: Participle clauses

1 Complete the sentences with the words in the box.

> having begun   believing   stealing
> having worked   stolen   begun
> working   having believed

1 _____ in 1970, the building took nearly ten years to complete.
2 _____ some cherries from his sister's plate, he ran outside.
3 _____ everything she said, he was shocked to discover the truth.
4 While _____ in Colombia, she met her husband and decided to stay there.
5 _____ to recover from his illness, he was able to start work again.
6 _____ in Japan for six years, she spoke excellent Japanese.
7 _____ that the house was empty, he began to search through all the drawers.
8 _____ over fifty years ago, the painting has finally been returned to its owner.

2 Are the sentences correct or incorrect? Cross out any mistakes and write the correct words at the end of the sentences.

1 Caught entering the building at night, the boys were taken to the police station. _____
2 Showered, we got dressed and went downstairs for dinner. _____
3 Was a friendly person, he decided to go and talk to the strangers. _____
4 Making from solid silver, the plate is extremely valuable. _____
5 After arguing all evening, the couple left the restaurant separately. _____
6 I'd like to meet some of the actors working on the show. _____
7 Walked all the way to the bank, we discovered it was closed. _____
8 While having taken a walk along the beach, he noticed a crowd near the pier. _____

VOCABULARY: Friendship and love

3 Complete the sentences with the correct forms of the words in the box.

> drift apart   hit it off   date   bond over
> soulmate   settle down   platonic

1 I met Tom in 2005, and we _____ our mutual love of surfing.
2 They had an intense, but _____, relationship that lasted for many years.
3 The first time I met my brother-in-law, we really didn't _____.
4 I don't think it's a great idea to _____ someone you work with.
5 When I met Grace, I realized that I had found my _____.
6 We were close at first, but, over the years, we began to _____.
7 She wanted to get married, but I wasn't ready to _____.

4 Fill in the blanks in the text with words describing friendship and love.

Bella and I go back ¹_____ _____ _____ – over twenty years, in fact. I first met her because I had a ²_____ on her brother Jake, so I started ³_____ out at their house as much as possible, hoping that he'd ask me out. Unfortunately for me, he'd already met his future girlfriend Julia at his karate club, and it was love at ⁴_____ _____ for him, so he barely noticed my interest. Still, Bella and I got along like a ⁵_____ _____ _____, and we're still very close today. We don't see ⁶_____ _____ _____ on everything (for example, our tastes in music could hardly be more different!), but if either of us is in trouble, we always know that the other one has our ⁷_____, and that's a great thing.

PRONUNCIATION: Intonation in participle clauses

5 ▶9.1 Read the sentences aloud, paying particular attention to the intonation before the comma. Listen and check.

1 Having expected to come in last in the race, he was thrilled with second place.
2 Loved by all her friends, she was one of the most popular students in her class.
3 Entering the room, she looked around her.
4 Noticing that the girl looked sad, he offered her some candy.
5 Abandoned by her parents, the girl was brought up by a local family.
6 Having decided to go camping, she bought herself a lightweight tent.

50

SKILLS 9B

READING: Locating specific information

1 Read the article. Which paragraph does each topic sentence belong to?

a However, the disadvantages are not insignificant.
b The rise of these "super-commuters" has been driven by two main factors.
c So how do couples make these arrangements work?
d Once upon a time, we believed that technology would free us from the cost and frustration of commuting.
e Such arrangements do have advantages.

Super-commuting – the enemy of good relationships?

1 _____ However, although a lucky few are able to pursue fulfilling careers from the comfort of their own homes, most of us are still expected to show up at the office and interact with one another or with our customers. And in our globalized world, "commuting" can be anything from a bus ride to the nearest town to the so-called NYLON commuters, who shuttle between New York and London, if not on a daily, then on a weekly or monthly basis.

2 _____ The first is the price of property in major employment hotspots. One real-estate agent estimates that every minute that we commute out of London saves around $3,500 on the price of a home. The second is the increase in short-term contracts. Parents do not want to expose their children to continual upheaval, with the disruption to their education that this would entail, even when it means, as it frequently does, that one parent ends up living away from home during the week or even for longer periods.

3 _____ Business executive Lisa Friedland lives and works in New York during the week, returning to her husband and young children on the weekends, and that works well for her. "I have the entire week to myself to concentrate on my work," she says. "But when I get on that train on Friday evening, I leave it all behind, and my family has 100% of my attention on the weekend."

4 _____ Spouses left at home may be resentful of having to do all the day-to-day chores themselves, while ones working far away can miss out, too. "It can be tough spending evenings in a hotel by yourself," says super-commuter Josh Miller. "You can't hold your baby or hug your wife digitally." In addition, reintegration into the family can be tricky. "When I'm away, I only have to think about myself, and I think that can make me a bit selfish," Miller admits.

5 _____ According to relationship coach Jan Powers, the key is good communication and commitment to a shared goal. "It's important that both parents – and the children if they are older – have signed on to the arrangement," she says. "It needs to work for all of you, not just the one whose career is benefiting."

2 Are the following statements true (T) or false (F)? Before you look for the answer, write the type of information you are looking for on the line below. Use the words in the box or your own ideas. For some questions, there may be more than one answer.

| amount   place   advice   reason   outcome |
| comparison   proper name   currency symbol |
| behavior |

1 More people work at home than work in an office. T / F
_____

2 NYLON commuters travel between the U.S. and the U.K. T / F
_____

3 It is cheaper to live in London than outside. T / F
_____

4 If children move often, their education may suffer. T / F
_____

5 Lisa Friedland likes being a super-commuter because she can work hard during the week. T / F
_____

6 One disadvantage is that both spouses end up doing more housework, etc. T / F
_____

7 Commuting does not have a negative effect on Josh Miller's family life. T / F
_____

8 It is important that everyone involved agrees to someone being a super-commuter. T / F
_____

3 Complete these sentences with a reflexive pronoun or *each other*. Then match sentences 1–5 with the functions of the pronouns a–e.

1 I looked up and there he was – the President _____! _____
2 Leo and James are friends, but they often annoy _____. _____
3 She tried to keep all the best food for _____. _____
4 Their boat looked very odd. I think they made it _____. _____
5 It's not good for you to sit in your room by _____ every evening. _____

a to show that something is reciprocal
b to show that something is done without help from anyone else
c to show that someone is alone
d to emphasize the subject of the sentence
e to show that something is for one person's use only

9C LANGUAGE

GRAMMAR: Past forms for unreal situations

1 Complete the sentences with the words and phrases in the box.

| had started | hadn't made | went | had brought |
| started | wouldn't make | would bring | had gone |

1 Look at those black clouds over there! I wish I _____ my umbrella!
2 I want to get a job, but my parents would rather I _____ to college.
3 It's about time you _____ earning your own money.
4 I didn't know you were bringing friends over for dinner. What if I _____ enough food?
5 Anna said the concert was amazing. If only I _____ with her!
6 I really like Adam's girlfriend. I wish he _____ her home more often.
7 I wish those kids _____ so much noise! They're really getting on my nerves.
8 I'm not very good at the violin. I wish I _____ learning when I was younger.

2 Complete the conversation with the correct form of the verbs in parentheses.

A I wish you ¹_____ (come) to Paris with us. We had such a great time!
B It sounded fantastic, but I couldn't afford it. If only I ²_____ (have) a better-paying job!
A Well, it's about time you ³_____ (find) one, in my opinion. They exploit you in that laboratory.
B I know, but I'll have finished my Ph.D. soon, and my supervisor would rather I ⁴_____ (stay) there for now because the work is so relevant to my studies. I wish they ⁵_____ (pay) me a bit more, though!
A What if you ⁶_____ (ask) them for a raise? Have you ever tried?
B Yes, I did, but they refused.
A What if you ⁷_____ (threaten) to leave? I bet they would have given you one then.
B To be honest, I wasn't confident enough to do that, but now I wish I ⁸_____ (have) the courage!

VOCABULARY: Commonly confused words

3 Are the underlined words in these sentences correct or incorrect?

                                Correct Incorrect

1 Prisoners shouldn't be allowed to profit from their crimes by writing books. ____ ____
2 We were stuck in stationery traffic for over an hour. ____ ____
3 She went to San Francisco to assist a conference. ____ ____
4 Talks broke down when the two sides were unable to reach a compromise. ____ ____
5 I sat besides Laura while she read the letter. ____ ____
6 I know that my fear of spiders isn't rationale. ____ ____
7 The others left, and, at last, I was alone in the building. ____ ____
8 If you know the answer, rise your hand. ____ ____

4 Complete the words.

1 The audience was divided into groups of those under 30 and those over. The la_____ group was asked to stand up.
2 They went out together for over five years, but didn't want the com_____ of marriage.
3 You will find paper, envelopes, and pens in the sta_____ closet.
4 A herb sauce would com_____ the fish perfectly.
5 He explained the rat_____ behind his new business strategy.
6 Polly said she was busy and would talk to us la_____.
7 The woman com_____ him on his new jacket.
8 That ring is very expensive, and, bes_____, you already have lots of nice rings.

PRONUNCIATION: Sentence stress

5 ▶9.2 Read the sentences aloud and underline the stressed words. Listen and check.

1 It's about time you called your parents.
2 If only I didn't have to go to work!
3 She'd rather we stayed in a hotel.
4 What if I hadn't seen you?
5 I wish we had more time.
6 If only the sun would shine!

SKILLS 9D

SPEAKING: Stating preference

1 ▶9.3 Listen to Philip and Bianca discussing a travel dilemma. Check (✓) the phrases they use.

1. Given the choice, I'd … ___
2. I'd just as soon … as … ___
3. I'd …, no doubt about it. ___
4. If I were you, I'd … ___
5. If it were up to me, I'd … ___
6. I'd much rather … than … ___
7. I guess … would be the best course of action. ___
8. If I were in your shoes, I'd … ___
9. Surely, it would be better to … ___
10. I'd prefer to … rather than … ___

2 ▶9.3 Listen again and complete the sentences.

1. The reason Bianca thinks Philip should choose Kenya is that he can _____ any time.
2. The reason Matt is looking forward to the hiking trip is that he hasn't been able to _____ for a long time.
3. Bianca tells an anecdote about going to visit her _____ in _____.
4. Philip stressed Matt's interest in Kenya by telling us that Matt studied _____ in college.
5. He adds that Matt has already spent time in _____.
6. Philip says he would _____ sightseeing with a friend.

3 Use your own ideas to add a sentence to support these opinions.

1. I'd just as soon walk as take a cab.
   _____
   _____
2. If it were up to me, I'd buy a second-hand laptop.
   _____
   _____
3. I'd prefer to live in a city rather than the country.
   _____
   _____
4. Surely, it would be better to change your job.
   _____
   _____
5. I'd much rather go to college next year than have a gap year.
   _____
   _____
6. Given the choice, I'd buy an electric car next time.
   _____
   _____

4 Complete the conversation with the phrases in exercise 1. There may be more than one correct answer.

A ¹_____ stay at home _____ go to Bill's party. It's going to be so boring.
B ²_____ definitely go. You never know who you might meet there.
A I don't feel very sociable today. ³_____ curl up with a good book _____ go out.
B ⁴_____ make the effort. Bill might be upset if you didn't go.
A ⁵_____ send Bill a text to say I'm not feeling very well _____ go to a boring party.
B ⁶_____ wouldn't do that. He saw you at lunchtime, and he knows you were fine then.
A ⁷_____ showing up late _____. That way, I've shown my face, but I won't have to stay too long.
B ⁸_____ go to the whole thing. I love parties!

53

9 REVIEW and PRACTICE

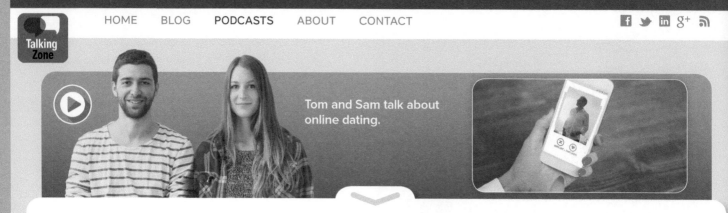

LISTENING

1 ▶ 9.4 Listen to the podcast and choose the correct options to complete the sentences.

1. Tom thinks dating is *more / less* romantic than it used to be.
2. Tom's parents *met by chance / planned their meeting*.
3. Tom thinks his parents *would / wouldn't* have started going out together if they'd used a dating app.
4. Sam *has / hasn't* used a dating app.
5. Tom's friend Freya first met her partner *online / in person*.
6. Sam's friends Will and Eva met *online / in person*.

2 ▶ 9.4 Listen again. Are the statements true (T), false (F), or doesn't say (DS)?

1. Sam thinks people should be more willing to take a chance in order to find a partner. ____
2. Tom's dad was sorry he didn't get Tom's mom's phone number when they met on the plane. ____
3. Tom's mom didn't think his dad would want to see her again. ____
4. Tom's mom was attracted to people who looked like his dad. ____
5. Tom thinks it's a good thing that dating apps give people so much choice. ____
6. Sam doesn't think that people should use dating apps. ____
7. Tom's friend Freya was an old friend of the man she was playing video games with. ____
8. Freya is now going out with the person she "killed" online. ____
9. Sam's friends Will and Eva were expecting to meet other people. ____
10. Will and Eva have now moved in together. ____

READING

1 Read Sam's blog on page 55 and check (✓) the things she talks about.

1. her relationship with Tom ____
2. what they do when they aren't working ____
3. Tom's attitude towards some of her friends ____
4. what she likes about her friend "X" ____
5. Tom's unpleasant behavior when he met "X" ____
6. a characteristic she likes her friends to have ____
7. what she dislikes about Tom's friend "Y" ____
8. the way "Y" behaves towards her ____

2 Read the blog again and choose the correct options to complete the sentences.

1. Sam and Tom
   a disagree about many important issues.
   b have similar opinions because they come from similar backgrounds.
   c have similar opinions about important things.
2. Sam says that Tom
   a tries to hide his dislike of her friends.
   b likes some of her friends.
   c finds some of her friends very boring.
3. Sam enjoys seeing "X" because she
   a likes the same kind of music as her.
   b has known her for a long time.
   c makes her reconsider the way she sees things.
4. Tom thinks that "X"
   a should listen to other people's opinions.
   b expresses her views too forcefully.
   c looks as though she might be violent.
5. Sam wants to be rude to "Y"
   a in order to make him stop being so polite.
   b because she doesn't like him.
   c because she wishes Tom wasn't friends with him.
6. Sam thinks that if she spent more time with Tom outside work,
   a they would be annoyed by each other's friends.
   b it would have a negative impact on their work.
   c they might become bored with each other.

REVIEW and PRACTICE 9

HOME **BLOG** PODCASTS ABOUT CONTACT

Sam writes about what she looks for in a friend.

"One man's meat is another man's poison"

One thing that's been puzzling me recently is why some of my closest friends seem to have friends that I don't get along with at all. And, of course, vice versa. This is definitely something that Tom and I have experienced.

As you know, not only do Tom and I work together, we're also extremely good friends. We don't see eye to eye on everything (our podcasts would be a bit tedious if we did!), but fundamentally, we share a worldview, and I trust him totally. If I'm having a bad day at work, I can rely on him to have my back, and I hope he feels the same about me.

But getting along as well as we do, it's strange that, by and large, we don't share the same group of friends outside work. In fact, Tom is downright uninterested in a couple of my best friends, and I have to admit that one guy he loves to hang out with bores me to tears! That got me thinking about what makes us "click" with certain people and not with others. Why is my idea of the ideal friend so different from Tom's?

Take my great friend "X." (I'm calling her that to protect Tom, though if she reads this, she'll probably recognize herself anyway!) I see "X" at least once a month, and, to be honest, I wish it was more often. We go back a long way. We initially bonded over a shared love of indie music, and I can't think of anyone I'd rather spend time with. She's so witty, and she often sees things from a different perspective to other people. I find her refreshing and stimulating, but when I introduced her to Tom, he shocked me the next day by saying, "If only 'X' didn't talk so much, she'd be very good company." It had never occurred to me to think of her that way. I only saw passion and enthusiasm, and someone willing to challenge lazy assumptions.

Thinking about it now, I realize that I like friends who will shock me a little bit. I tire pretty quickly of people who are too nice, like Tom's friend "Y." "Y" is charming, and he's a kind and loyal friend to Tom, but I just wish he wasn't so polite all the time! I'd much rather people pushed me out of my comfort zone just a little. It's shameful, I know, but whenever I meet him, I have to fight off this terrible urge to insult him, just to get some kind of reaction. I want to say to him, "Don't you ever get mad? Don't you ever say anything mean? Can't you just, for once, say something that isn't utterly predictable?"

I find it hard to understand what Tom sees in "Y," and clearly he feels the same about "X." I guess it just comes down to the fact that we want different things from our friends. And, besides, it's probably a good thing that we don't socialize together too much outside of work, or our wonderful relationship could get a bit stale. As everyone knows, you can have too much of a good thing!

UNIT 10 Being human

10A LANGUAGE

GRAMMAR: Distancing language

1 Do these sentences contain distancing language? If yes, underline the distancing language.

	Yes	No
1 Experts estimated that there were only about 300 of these animals left.	___	___
2 His explanation was believed by everyone who heard it.	___	___
3 The company was reported to be in financial difficulty.	___	___
4 This isn't her best movie, according to my sister.	___	___
5 My piano teacher says that to improve, it is essential to practice every day.	___	___
6 Apparently, he was a kind, hardworking man.	___	___
7 Sally seemed to be a little upset earlier.	___	___
8 The thieves are thought to have broken in through a window.	___	___

2 Are the sentences correct or incorrect? Cross out any mistakes and write the correct words at the end of the sentences.

1 The woman is believed to travel to Peru. _____
2 In those days, such activities were thought to be inappropriate for women. _____
3 Apparently, the road will be closed on Sunday. _____
4 This medicine thinks to be more effective for children. _____
5 According our records, nobody by that name has been here. _____
6 The number of people affected is reported around 200. _____
7 It appears that Mel has forgotten about our meeting. _____
8 It is said to be poisonous snakes in this region. _____

VOCABULARY: Humans and self

3 Complete the sentences with the words in the box.

> self-esteem   human resources   selfless   self-employed
> humane   self-sufficient   human being   humanitarian

1 My daughter is only 10, but she's already very _____.
2 He's the manager of the _____ department.
3 The ability to make moral decisions is an essential part of being a _____.
4 They traveled on a _____ mission to bring food to the refugees.
5 Years of criticism from his parents left him with very low _____.
6 _____ workers don't have paid vacations.
7 She had a _____ desire to help others.
8 When animals have to be killed, we use the most _____ methods possible.

4 Replace the underlined phrases with a word containing *human* or *self*.

1 You shouldn't be surprised if people are greedy. It's just the way most people are.
2 Standing there on the stage, I felt very aware that everyone was looking at me.
3 Of course, they can lose weight. They just need a bit of the ability to control themselves.
4 The way these prisoners have been treated is absolutely unlike the way any person should behave.
5 We are fighting for things every person should have, such as food, housing, and freedom of speech.
6 She was accused of hitting the man, but claimed she had acted out of the need to protect herself.
7 They produced some of the greatest art in the history of all the people in the world.
8 I know he's had a hard time, but feeling sorry for himself isn't going to make things better.

PRONUNCIATION: Emphasizing uncertainty

5 ▶10.1 Read the sentences aloud and underline the words that are stressed to emphasize uncertainty. Listen and check.

1 It is believed that thousands of people will attend the protest.
2 She's too busy to come with us, apparently.
3 The boys are thought to have traveled to Boston.
4 According to my parents, there used to be a windmill here.
5 It appears that his plan was successful.
6 It seems that you need to pay to enter the museum.

SKILLS 10B

LISTENING: Understanding precise and imprecise numbers

1 ▶10.2 Listen to Nick and Hannah talking about population size.

Are they talking about

a present-day population numbers?
b historical population numbers?

2 ▶10.2 Listen again. Answer the following questions. Write the whole phrase including any language that shows whether the number is precise or imprecise.

1 How many people in the world are Chinese?
_____
2 What is the population density of Russia?
_____
3 What is the population density of the U.S.?
_____
4 What proportion of the world's population lives in China?
_____
5 How many people live in China?
_____
6 What is the population of the world?
_____
7 How many births had there been up until August in the year of this conversation?
_____
8 How many deaths had there been in the same period?
_____

3 ▶10.3 Read the sentences aloud. Underline the places where a /d/ or /t/ sound at the end of a word could be dropped. Listen and check.

1 China isn't the largest country in the world.
2 Russia is one of the least densely populated countries.
3 People tend to overestimate the extent to which the countryside is disappearing.
4 U.S. records show that only around 3% of land is built on.
5 There's a website that shows how fast the population is growing.
6 We might be able to overcome the problem of rapid population growth if each couple had no more than two children.

4 Complete the sentences by adding the prefixes *re-*, *over-* or *mis-* to the words in the box and using them in their correct forms.

| charge (x 2) | store | create | juvenate | interpret |
| understand | treat | behave | come | |

1 Rick has had to _____ a lot of problems in order to become the successful businessperson he is today.
2 The vintage car was very damaged when we found it, but we have now _____ it to its original state.
3 She threatened to punish the children if they _____, in any way, during the ceremony.
4 The chicken dish was so delicious, I tried to _____ it at home, but with little success.
5 I think the store _____ me for the things I bought there.
6 I'm sorry, I _____ you. I thought you said the tickets were $10 each.
7 She was fined for _____ the dogs and prohibited from keeping animals in her home.
8 She had been feeling tired, but her trip to the beach _____ her somewhat.
9 Should I throw these batteries away, or can you _____ them?
10 It was only a joke, but she _____ it as a serious comment and was really offended.

10C LANGUAGE

GRAMMAR: Adverbs and adverbial phrases

1 Are the adverbs in the correct places in these sentences? Cross out any mistakes, write ^ where the adverb should go, and write it above the line.

1 I'm so hungry! **Really** I need to eat soon.

2 I'm going to get together with Jamie **tomorrow**.

3 I **secretly** arranged to meet her the next day.

4 He grabbed **eagerly** the rope and pulled himself up.

5 They saw that the train had **to their horror** just left.

6 **Very rarely** he sells any of his work.

7 I noticed **on top of the roof** a large bird.

8 I **reluctantly** agreed to accompany her to the party.

2 Choose the correct options to complete the sentences.

1 I _____ assumed that food would be provided.
  a wrong   b wrongly

2 She tripped on a stone and _____ fell.
  a near   b nearly

3 They showed up _____ for the meeting.
  a late   b lately

4 We couldn't talk _____ while our boss was there.
  a free   b freely

5 Make sure you divide the money _____.
  a fair   b fairly

6 Make sure you hit the ball _____.
  a hard   b hardly

7 The TV was working _____ yesterday.
  a fine   b finely

8 I found his stories _____ entertaining.
  a high   b highly

9 What we need _____ is a place to live.
  a most   b mostly

10 The jewels were _____ believed to have come from India.
  a wide   b widely

VOCABULARY: Adverb collocations

3 Choose the correct options to complete the sentences.

1 The crash left several people *strongly / seriously / deeply* injured.

2 Housing here is *strongly / utterly / unbelievably* expensive.

3 I *vaguely / mildly / potentially* remember meeting her some years ago.

4 The way he spoke to me was *downright / strongly / severely* rude.

5 I turned the job down, but later I *potentially / incredibly / bitterly* regretted my decision.

6 I know that he feels *widely / severely / deeply* ashamed of his actions.

7 These customs are *strongly / deeply / widely* observed in our country.

8 It's *utterly / bitterly / highly* pointless telling her anything.

4 Choose an adverb from box A and an adjective from box B to complete the sentences. Use each word only once.

A	highly widely incredibly mildly seriously bitterly potentially utterly

B	hot likely amusing damaged known damaging unbelievable disappointed

1 We need to avoid any _____ stories getting to the media.

2 It gets _____ here in the summer.

3 I thought the movie was _____, but not nearly as funny as people claim.

4 He was _____ about failing his exams.

5 She wasn't injured, but her car was _____.

6 The politician is _____ for his passionate speaking style.

7 The story about the president's wife is _____.

8 She's very well qualified, so it's _____ that she'll get the job.

PRONUNCIATION: Word stress

5 ▶ 10.4 Read the sentences aloud and underline the stressed syllable in the words in **bold**. Listen and check.

1 **Apparently**, they're moving to the U.K.

2 The report **severely** criticized her leadership.

3 I found their behavior **utterly** astonishing.

4 We **carefully** removed all the packaging.

5 They realized they were **hopelessly** lost.

6 Most people we met were **incredibly** friendly.

SKILLS 10D

WRITING: Summarizing data

1 Look at the graph and read the summary. Underline the words and phrases used to show trends (e.g., increases, decreases, rates of change, similarities, or differences).

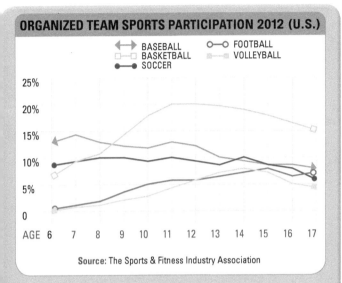

The chart above shows levels of participation for children in the U.S. in a variety of sports. It can be seen clearly that basketball is the most frequently played sport, showing a sharp increase from the age of 6 and peaking between the ages of 11 and 12. One possible reason for this is that basketball is very accessible. All that is needed is a hoop and a ball. In addition, it tends to be popular with both sexes and all ethnic groups.

In contrast to the other sports covered in the graph, neither football nor volleyball are played by the youngest children, due to their insufficient physical maturity. However, by the age of 17, football has overtaken soccer, though only by a tiny margin. Soccer has the most constant level of participation across the entire age range, starting at around 7.5% and ending at around 6%, with its highest level of around 10% occurring between the ages of 8–12, presumably because it is a universally popular sport that can be played almost anywhere and at any level.

Another striking trend is that the majority of sports show a gradual decline starting at the age of 14. This may be due to a variety of factors, such as increased academic demands or lower levels of parental control over leisure choices. The only exception to this trend is football, which shows a slight increase between 14 and 15, but then also falls off somewhat.

In conclusion, while all sports have significant participation rates among children and teens, and all of them (with the exception of volleyball) still have participation rates of 5% or more at the age of 17, basketball remains, by far, the most popular sport, at just over 15% for children aged 9–17.

2 What reasons are given for the following?
1. the popularity of basketball
2. the fact that 6-year-olds don't play football or volleyball
3. the popularity of soccer
4. the decrease in participation in sports after the age of 14

3 Look at the graph below. Are the sentences true (T) or false (F)?
1. In rural areas, boys participating in organized sports outnumber girls in all age groups.
2. Involvement in organized sports decreases for both sexes as students get older.
3. At ages 8–11, the highest level of participation for boys is in urban areas.
4. Between the ages of 8–11 and ages 11–14, the participation levels for both sexes decline in all areas.
5. Fewer girls than boys living in suburban areas take part in organized sports in all age groups.

4 Which sentences could provide reasons for the numbers in the graph? Circle the cautious language in each sentence.
1. Parents in suburban areas, more than in rural areas, appear to encourage their children to take part in sports.
2. In urban areas, boys aged 11–14 tend to spend more time playing computer games than their counterparts in rural areas.
3. The sharp fall in participation levels for girls aged 14–17 in urban areas might be due to the pressure on them to concentrate more on their studies.
4. Presumably, boys aged 14–17 get more involved in sports in suburban areas than in rural ones because there are fewer athletic sports in small towns.

5 Write a summary to accompany the graph.
- Describe the main trends.
- Give possible explanations.
- Use cautious language.

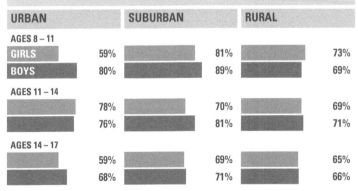

59

10 REVIEW and PRACTICE

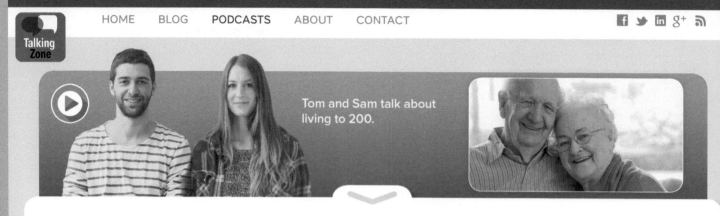

LISTENING

1 ▶ 10.5 Listen to the podcast and number a–f in the order that you hear them (1–6).

a the number of extremely old people in the world at the moment ____
b an animal that lives to a very old age ____
c how people feel about having grandchildren ____
d studying the way genes influence the age we live to ____
e the effect of extreme old age on marriages ____
f a philosopher's view on death ____

2 ▶ 10.5 Listen again. Who makes the following points: Tom (T), Sam (S), or neither of them (N)?

1 Someone who is alive now might live to be 200. ____
2 Seeing how the world develops over a long period of time would be enjoyable. ____
3 The knowledge that life is short encourages us to do things. ____
4 If we lived to 200, our families would be much too big. ____
5 There may be a limit on how long it is possible to live. ____
6 Advances in our knowledge of genetics may enable us to increase our lifespan. ____
7 Scientists can already reverse the aging process in mice to a certain extent. ____
8 The world couldn't sustain a population that lived to 200. ____
9 Research on bowhead whales has helped scientists improve health in elderly humans. ____
10 The idea of being married for 170 years would not appeal to people. ____

READING

1 Read Tom's blog on page 61 and choose the best summary.

a Tom wonders why he and his brother are so different. His friend Heidi, who is a psychologist, explains that both nature and nurture are important and tells him about the effect of epigenetics.
b Tom wishes that he and his brother were more alike and asks his friend Heidi to explain why they are not. Heidi tells him that epigenetics have caused the physical differences that make them so different.
c Tom wants to know why his personality is so different from his brother's. He learns that his brother's brain is physically different from his own because of the different way their parents behaved towards them.

2 Are the sentences true (T), false (F), or doesn't say (DS)?

1 It annoys Tom when his brother plays the same notes many times. ____
2 Tom and his brother have significantly different backgrounds. ____
3 Adam is very introverted and doesn't go out with his friends. ____
4 Adam is a good violinist. ____
5 Adam would like to do Tom's job. ____
6 "Nativists" think that nature is far more important than nurture. ____
7 Scientists have used pairs of twins to study the question of nature versus nurture. ____
8 Scientists are now certain that criminal behavior is caused by genes. ____
9 Scientists have identified physical changes caused by epigenetics. ____
10 Epigenetics only affects people during childhood. ____

REVIEW and PRACTICE 10

HOME   BLOG   PODCASTS   ABOUT   CONTACT

Tom asks whether nature or nurture influences our personalities more.

Nature or nurture?

I have to admit I've always subscribed to the view that most people are the product of their environments, and that where, and how, you are brought up exerts the biggest influence over your personality. But that doesn't explain how people in the same family often turn out to be so different. Take my brother Adam and me, for example.

Last weekend, I was at my parents' house. I was watching TV with my dad, but was vaguely aware of my brother practicing his violin in the other room, going over the same notes again and again, tens – if not hundreds – of times, and the question that has struck me so many times before popped into my head again. Why is Adam so different from me? How is it that two people who look quite similar, who share the same genetic mix, and endured the same upbringing (only joking, Mom and Dad!), could end up with personalities that are so utterly different?

Whereas I'm an extrovert and a bit of a loudmouth, Adam is much quieter. I'm not saying he's a nerd, and he does have a social life, but he's equally happy spending hours on end reading books or perfecting his bowing technique. I'd never have the self-discipline for that sort of repetitive activity, but then, unlike him, I'm not a member of an elite amateur orchestra. And, on the other hand, although he's not lacking in self-esteem, he'd be far too self-conscious to bare his soul on a public podcast or blog, the way Sam and I do all the time!

Anyway, this time I decided to go a bit further than my usual idle speculation, so I contacted my old school friend Heidi, who's now working as a psychologist. I wanted to know the current thinking on nature versus nurture. What makes my brother and me so different?

From what she told me, it appears that most scientists have moved away from the more extreme positions of the past, when so-called "nativists" believed that all our characteristics were passed down via our parents, while "environmentalists" insisted we were born as a blank sheet of paper and developed only in response to the experiences we had. Apparently, studies of twins and adopted children carried out in the 1990s suggest that nature and nurture have roughly equal influence.

There is also currently a huge interest in DNA research, and debate rages over whether it will be possible to identify genes for traits such as criminality, addiction, or intelligence. Heidi also told me about a fascinating area that I'd never even heard of before – something called "epigenetics." According to scientists, this is when things in our environment physically change the way a gene is expressed. She gave the example of a child who might have a genetic tendency towards aggression. If the parents respond to his difficult behavior with aggression themselves, epigenetics can cause the child's brain to actually develop differently, potentially worsening the problem in a physical way.

It's all pretty mind-boggling stuff, but I guess the lesson from it is that since so many factors, both genetic and environmental, contribute to making us who we are, the fact that Adam and I are so unalike isn't really as surprising as I thought it was.

WRITING PRACTICE

WRITING: Writing a proposal

A _____

The first recommendation would be to create a small snack bar in the library. We envision it as a simple store, selling a limited range of hot and cold drinks, in addition to cookies and cakes. It might be worth renting the needed equipment at first. It would be advisable to arrange seating away from the books to avoid damage from spills. By offering drinks and light snacks, we hope to entice visitors who might otherwise stay away from the library. It is worth noting that since the closure of the Black Cat Diner in 2016, there are no coffee shops or small restaurants in the vicinity.

We also suggest establishing a community movie theater, screening a movie every two to three weeks, possibly followed by a short discussion after each movie. This initiative would require investment in equipment and the installation of black-out facilities. We suggest charging a small entrance fee to cover the cost of renting the movies and paying any licensing fees.

B _____

307 users responded. The overwhelming majority indicated preferences for two options:
- a snack bar
- a community movie theater

C _____

Maple Street Library presently attracts just under 200 visitors a day, compared with 350 in 2017. This steep decline reflects a nationwide phenomenon. However, there is evidence that this trend can be slowed down, if not reversed, with the introduction of additional services that are appropriate for the local community. To ascertain what additional services would be attractive to our community, we recently e-mailed a survey to library users.

D _____

We acknowledge that investment is required to implement these recommendations. However, we are confident that the initial expenditure would, over time, be recouped through food and drink sales and through ticket sales. Additionally, we strongly believe that the offering of these services would greatly increase Maple Street Library's popularity.

E _____

The aim of this proposal is to suggest ways in which we can increase interest in this very valuable local resource. We are deeply concerned that the decrease in visitors in the last two years may lead to cuts in city funding for the library, perhaps even resulting in its closure.

---

1 The paragraphs in this proposal are in the wrong order. Match the headings in the box with paragraphs A–E and indicate the correct order (1–5) of the paragraphs.

> Conclusion   Current situation   Introduction
> Recommendations   Feedback

1 ___   2 ___   3 ___   4 ___   5 ___

2 Read the proposal again and find more formal words that have the same meaning as the underlined words or phrases in these sentences.

1 We <u>expect</u> that the project will start in 2020. (paragraph A)
2 Currently there are few attractions to <u>encourage</u> people to come to the area. (paragraph A)
3 An <u>enormous</u> majority voted in favor of the proposal. (paragraph B)
4 <u>At the moment</u> we have six permanent staff members. (paragraph C)
5 Did they <u>discover</u> what was causing the problem? (paragraph C)
6 We hope to <u>carry out</u> our research project during the course of the year. (paragraph D)
7 Most people surveyed said that they had benefited <u>a lot</u> from this resource. (paragraph D)
8 We are <u>very</u> concerned about the situation (paragraph E)

3 Rewrite these recommendations so that they are less direct, using "softening" expressions and verb forms.

1 Our suggestion is to extend our hours.
   _____

2 You should lower the ticket price so that it is more affordable. _____
   _____

3 Another idea is to consult customers on the issue. _____
   _____

4 Expand the range of dishes that you offer to include more vegetarian options. _____
   _____

5 Consider taking on more staff to deal with busy periods. _____
   _____

4 Imagine you are a member of an Arts Center Advisory Group. You feel that the center does not cater sufficiently to young people. Write a proposal with your suggestions. Your proposal should be organized into the paragraph types mentioned in exercise 1, use "softened" recommendations, and appropriate formal language.

WRITING PRACTICE

WRITING: Opinion and discussion essays

Is the weakening of family ties bad for society?

1. A recent study in the U.S. showed that millennials are much less likely than their parents to count a family member among their closest friends. ¹_____ include the fact that modern life creates both a psychological and a physical distance between family members, with more and more young adults going away to college or taking jobs in distant cities – and increasingly in faraway countries.

2. ²_____ there can be advantages to this situation, with the exciting opportunities and greater freedom that it offers, there are definite disadvantages, too. One drawback is that our mobile lifestyle means societies are no longer as stable as they once were. Not only do we not have our parents and siblings living nearby, many of us do not even know our neighbors, and ³_____ that we both offer less support to them and receive less support from them.

3. ⁴_____, without their families nearby, new parents struggle to cope with juggling childcare and work. Grandparents, aunts, and uncles miss out, too, as day-care staff takes on roles that would once have been theirs. ⁵_____, at the other end of life, our elderly relatives are spending their last months or years in nursing homes, cared for by strangers, instead of their own families.

4. ⁶_____, family bonds are weakened by these developments, and this is damaging to our society. Families should provide the structure that holds society together. As the old saying goes, "blood is thicker than water," and we should, ⁷_____, try to find ways to enable families to stay together more. ⁸_____, you can't be really close to people you only see a few times a year.

1 Read the essay and fill in the blanks with the linking words or phrases in the box.

> in addition   after all   although
> in conclusion   similarly   the result is
> therefore   reasons for this

2 Read the essay again and answer the questions.
1. Does the author believe that the weakening of family ties is bad for society? _____
2. Does he/she acknowledge any opposing viewpoints? _____
3. Find two synonyms in paragraph 1 that mean "a long way away." _____ _____
4. Find two synonyms in paragraph 2 that mean "something that causes problems." _____
5. Find a summary noun in the first line of paragraph 2. _____
6. Find a summary noun in the first line of paragraph 4. _____
7. What is the author's recommendation for the future?
_____

3 Choose pairs of synonyms from the box to complete the sentences.

> values   ties   obligation   beliefs and opinions
> embarrassing   siblings   select   connections
> brothers and sisters   duty   choose   awkward

1. We are free to _____ our friends, whereas we cannot _____ our family members.
2. Sometimes it can be _____ to discuss personal problems with family members. With friends, it is less _____.
3. The shared identity we have with our _____ creates a strong bond. After all, our _____ had the same upbringing as us, so they understand our past.
4. Unlike family, when it comes to friends, it is not their _____ to care for us, and this lack of _____ makes their support even more valuable.
5. Our friends are likely to have similar _____ to us, whereas family members, especially those from other generations, may have very different _____.
6. Within families, there are strong _____ that go back to birth. Our _____ with friends can never truly be as deep.

4 Write an opinion or discussion essay on the topic below.

Are family members more important than friends?
- Structure your essay with an introduction, two paragraphs in the main body, and a conclusion.
- Use cohesive devices such as synonyms, reference words, summary nouns, and linking words.

WRITING PRACTICE

WRITING: Summarizing data

1 Look at the graph. Read the accompanying text and fill in blanks 1–7 with phrases a–g.

a largest difference
b substantial drop
c rose continually
d steady increase
e narrowed
f remained even
g consistently

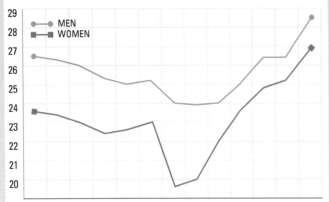

Median age of marriage in the U.S. from 1890 to 2010
Source: The United States Census Bureau

This chart shows the median age at which people in the U.S. got married from 1890 to 2010. The two most striking trends are the ¹_____ in marriage age between 1940 and 1950, and the fact that it ²_____ until 2010 for women and either ³_____ or rose for men.

The ⁴_____ in marriage age beginning in 1970 has several probable reasons. One is that many more young people were delaying marriage in favor of a college education. Towards the end of the twentieth century, couples frequently lived together before marriage without the social stigma that would have prevented such arrangements previously. It is likely that the trend towards smaller families also played a part: with fewer children, parenthood could be delayed somewhat.

It can clearly be seen that men have ⁵_____ married at a later age than women, almost certainly due to social convention. However, that gap ⁶_____ beginning in 1970. The ⁷_____ in age was around 1950, although it is noteworthy that both sexes married younger at that point. It would appear that this desire for the stability of marriage was a reaction to the trauma and uncertainty of the Second World War.

In conclusion, it seems that marriage age is strongly influenced by external political and social factors, rather than being the result of romantic impulses.

2 Look at the graph below and complete the sentences.

1 The most significant change during this period is _____.

2 In contrast to women, _____

3 There are different scales for mothers and fathers because _____

3 Rewrite the statements to make them sound more cautious.

1 Families cannot afford for one parent to stay at home.
_____

2 Men earn more than women.
_____

3 More women are now in high-paying jobs, so it makes financial sense for their husbands to stay at home.
_____

4 Society still expects mothers to care for children.
_____

5 It is now more socially acceptable for men to stay at home with children.
_____

4 Write a commentary to accompany this graph.
- Describe the main trends.
- Give possible explanations, using sentences from exercise 2 or your own ideas.

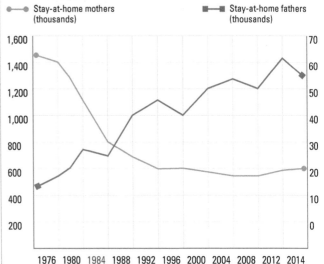

Number of Canadian stay-at-home mothers and fathers with at least one child under 16, 1976 to 2014
Source: Statistics Canada, Labor Force Survey, 1976 to 2014